Stewardship

STARTS AT HOME

USING GOD'S GIFTS TO GROW AS DISCIPLES
OF CHRIST IN OUR DOMESTIC CHURCH

LISA McARDLE

Catholic Stewardship Consultants, Inc.
CatholicSteward.com

Stewardship STARTS AT HOME:

Using God's Gifts to Grow as Disciples of Christ in Our Domestic Church

Publisher's address and contact information:
Catholic Stewardship Consultants, Inc.,
4325 Washington Road, Evans, GA 30809

Printed in the United States of America

Edited By: Rob Mueller
Book Cover Design: Joanna Graham and Hunter Amberson

First Edition: March 2022

ISBN 978-0-578-35884-0

To my husband, Eric,
who always leads our family
in a relentless pursuit of holiness.

And, to all the priests we have encountered
along the way who have encouraged us, prayed
for us, loved us, challenged us, and inspired us,
as we walk the Stewardship Way of Life.

Contents

Foreword

Even with so many experts offering ways to raise a family these days, seldom are these suggestions universally applicable or effective. Embracing a life of stewardship, especially for families who seek to follow Christ, does actually work in every instance, because stewardship starts with the unique gifts of each family member, given by God, for good.

The thoughtful reflections in this book prove that Lisa McArdle has worked faithfully at finding foolproof ways for her family to respond to the Good News of Jesus Christ. Her insights provide helpful tips and a powerful theological foundation for any family to find the way to the heavenly Kingdom together through Christ.

Retreat conferences and workshops on Stewardship in the Family have led to the give-and-take that makes good ideas powerful, prudent, and possible. Realizing that stewardship is truly the disciple's response can honestly direct the good we strive to do in our families.

Spend some time with the wisdom of Lisa McArdle as you read this book. Be ready to be challenged, supported, and awakened to better family life for you and those you love.

— Fr. Godfrey Mullen

Rector, Saint Benedict Cathedral, Evansville, Ind.
Benedictine Monk of Saint Meinrad Archabbey

THE BOOK
CHILDREN READ

Being part of a family is one of life's greatest blessings. And, as parents, grandparents, foster parents, spiritual parents, we are called to be the primary faith formers of our children and grandchildren.

Paragraph 2223 of the *Catechism of the Catholic Church* states: "Parents have the first responsibility for the education of their children. They bear witness to this responsibility first by creating a home where tenderness, forgiveness, respect, fidelity, and disinterested service are the rule. The home is well suited for education in the virtues. This requires an apprenticeship in self-denial, sound judgment, and self-mastery—the preconditions of all true freedom. Parents should teach their children to subordinate the 'material and instinctual dimensions to interior and spiritual ones.' Parents have a grave responsibility to give good examples to their children. By knowing how to acknowledge their own failings to their children, parents will be better able to guide and correct them."

Saint Augustine's quote nails the essence of this essential duty: "The life of the parents is the book which the children read."

Have you ever stopped to think about what type of "book" you read growing up in your family or what type of "book" your children and grandchildren are currently reading?

After all, it is in the mundane, day-to-day tasks that we—parents and grandparents—unveil our priorities. It is our actions (not our words) that permeate our children as they observe our movements—both good and bad. We can demonstrate unconditional love that they will emulate and an openness to ongoing forgiveness that they will repeat. Ultimately our daily choices build the initial layer of faith formation in our families.

If there was a report card for this, what grade would you give yourself?

"THE LIFE OF THE PARENTS IS THE BOOK WHICH THE *children* READ."

— SAINT AUGUSTINE

"THE MOST SIGNIFICANT
CHALLENGE FACING
THE CATHOLIC CHURCH
TODAY IS THE

attrition

OF OUR OWN PEOPLE."

———

— BISHOP ROBERT BARRON

One

FLEEING OF OUR (ONCE) FAITHFUL

According to Bishop Robert Barron—the founder of *Word on Fire Catholic Ministries* and Auxiliary Bishop of the Archdiocese of Los Angeles—for every one person joining our church today, six are leaving. He goes on to explain that most young people today identify with what he refers to as the "Generation of Nones," or those who claim to have no religious affiliation at all.

The *Gallup 2020 Church Pew Survey* solidifies Bishop Barron's findings and uncovered that currently, 31 percent of millennials have no religious affiliation, which is up from 22 percent a decade ago. Similarly, 33 percent of the portion of Generation Z that has reached adulthood have no religious preference either.

Furthermore, Gallup found that each generation has seen a decline in church membership among those who do affiliate with a specific religion. These declines have ranged between six and eight points over the past two decades for traditionalists, baby boomers, and Generation Xers who identify with a religious faith. In just the past 10 years, the share of religious millennials who are church members has declined from 63 percent to 50 percent.

Specifically for Catholics, Bishop Barron states that one-third of people raised Catholic no longer identify as Catholic today. These people grew up in Catholic households, received the sacraments, and many even attended parochial school. Yet, they claim to feel an emptiness, lack a genuine understanding of Jesus, and at their depths, feel disconnected from their Catholic upbringing.

Why, despite parental efforts, has this "Generation of Nones" pulled away?

There are many reasons why young people leave the Catholic faith. According to the 2020 *Gallup Pew Survey on Religion*, they leave because they have drifted away from the religion, stopped believing in the religion's teachings, feel their spiritual needs are not being met, are unhappy with teachings about the Bible, are dissatisfied with the atmosphere at worship services, and feel there are too many asks for money, etc.

For those who choose to remain active Catholics, however, there does appear to be one underlying element: a personal relationship with Jesus.

Those young Catholics who have gone beyond the formalities, beyond the liturgical boxes to check off, and beyond the "have-tos" to foster a genuine connection with Jesus are the ones who have remained firmly planted in the Catholic Church. A Church where they can live out their faith with the Mass and the Eucharist, the sacraments, and active participation in ministry and parish life. They *want* to stay.

So, how do we ensure our children and grandchildren remain faith-filled Catholics who benefit from an authentic relationship with Jesus? How do we take it a step beyond the obvious channels of going to Mass and receiving the sacraments?

Of course, there are no guarantees. There is no surefire plan to succeed.

However, after almost three decades of working with Catholic churches around the country, I have found a common denominator—an indicator of how vibrant, young Catholics shine and appear to be the antithesis of the "Generation of Nones." There is no geographical denominator. There is no financial indicator. There is no racial indicator. There is no academic indicator.

The common denominator is that these young people are from families that consistently live out the call to stewardship and discipleship 24 hours a day, seven days a week, year-round.

The families that live a "Stewardship Way of Life" produce a genuine connection with Jesus, with the understanding that all the blessings we have in this life are freely given to us by God, and that out of gratitude we are called to share those gifts with all those we encounter. There is nothing extraordinary about these families—only a commitment to live out the call of stewardship and holiness in their homes. It is who they are.

And, if you were baptized, it's a call you have received, too.

SAINTLY INSPIRATIONS

So, do you have doubts that you have received this special call? Let's look to the saints for some inspiration.

Have you ever stopped to think about who is your favorite saint? I bet you have one... or more than one. I know I do. After all, there are so many incredible superheroes for Christ.

As a young girl, my favorite saint was Saint Joan of Arc. Aside from admiring her cool fighting armor (and, let's face it, what young girl doesn't like to dress up?), her courage, and her willingness to fight for Jesus at whatever cost inspired me. Being a girl and having a female superhero was convicting. Joan of Arc is impressive, especially to my young girl self.

Then, as I grew older, I heard the story of Saint Paul's conversion. Wow! I imagined him on the Road to Damascus, falling off his horse, hearing a voice, and then going blind, having the whole trajectory of his life altered in that split second. Regaining his eyesight only to do the opposite of his original mission—rooting for Christians instead of persecuting them. When I visited Rome in May 2013, and as I stood in the magnificent Papal Basilica of Saint Paul Outside the Walls, I was reminded of the powerful encouragement I receive when I consider Saint Paul's story. I want to be like Saint Paul too.

More recently, as I continue to enjoy learning more about history—particularly World War II history—I stumbled upon Saint Maximilian Kolbe. Stranded in the dreaded Auschwitz-Birkenau concentration camp, he does the unthinkable and offers to be put to death instead of another camp victim. Fearlessly and faithfully, he puts others before himself unto his very death. Would I be able to do likewise if I were in the same situation?

Let's face it. Saints can be intimidating. They do amazing and unbelievable acts out of love. In the most terrifying situations, they put aside their own concerns and fears to selflessly serve their fellow brothers and sisters in Christ.

Certainly, these are capabilities that only "saints" have, right? I am only Lisa McArdle, mother of five and grandmother of two. I clearly can't expect the same of myself.

Yet, the call that the saints received is the very same call that I receive. And that you receive.

This "Call to Holiness" isn't just reserved for the saints, the pope, the archbishops and bishops, the rectors and pastors, the deacons and brothers, the sisters, the monks, and the consecrated singles that we know. Furthermore, this call isn't just intended for those few select friends who seem to have their spiritual lives in perfect order. You know the ones. We all have some in our lives. The ones we could never be like.

Although the Call to Holiness is in fact for them, it is also meant for you and me. It's meant for all of us.

"IF YOU WANT TO
BRING HAPPINESS
INTO THE WORLD

go home

AND LOVE YOUR
FAMILY."

———

— SAINT MOTHER TERESA OF CALCUTTA

Two

SAINT MOTHER TERESA'S GENTLE WAYS

When we consider Saint Mother Teresa, she doesn't have the same gory story as many of the saints and martyrs we learn about. She wasn't beheaded, stoned to death, or thrown in a den with lions. Yet, to me, Mother Teresa's story seems even more powerful.

She is credited with one particular quote that I love so much it is hanging on the wall in my office.

It reads: "If you want to Bring Happiness into the World, Go Home and Love your Family."

Now, to be honest, when I first read this quote, I thought it was a bit of a cop-out. I mean, I already love my family. Likely, you all love your families too. Clearly, there is something bigger we can do for Christ. If we want to roll up our sleeves and make a difference in the world, this statement seems so "blah" or "boring" in comparison to the fearless feats done by other saints.

Yet, through the years, I changed my mind and realized Saint Mother Teresa was far wiser than I will ever be, and that is why she is already a saint for all of us to emulate. Saint Mother Teresa knew that peace and love in our homes were essential ingredients to bringing Christ's love to the world. After all, the family is the foundation for all religious formation and sanctification. It's where we learn how to treat others, to love others, and to forgive others—starting with our parents, our siblings, and then moving on to our spouses, children, and grandchildren. If the chain of peace and love continued to sprinkle out into the world there would be a beautiful combustion of harmony worldwide. And, if we all did those things, wouldn't there be peace everywhere? Clearly, Saint Mother Teresa knew that forming disciples begins in our homes.

The Call to Holiness that Saint Mother Teresa and all of the saints received is a call for you. And it's a call for me. If your ultimate goal in this world is to reach eternal life with God in heaven (and who of us isn't aiming for that?), then responding to that call is critical.

You may ask how? How is it that we respond to the Call to Holiness? How do we enter into deeper holiness for ourselves and for our families? How do we grow as disciples to follow this call?

It's simple. We respond to the call of discipleship through living a life of stewardship.

"STEWARDSHIP IS THE
GRATEFUL RESPONSE OF
A CHRISTIAN DISCIPLE
WHO RECOGNIZES AND
RECEIVES GOD'S GIFTS
AND SHARES THESE GIFTS
generously
IN LOVE OF
GOD AND NEIGHBOR."

— UNITED STATES CONFERENCE OF CATHOLIC BISHOPS'
PASTORAL LETTER, *STEWARDSHIP: A DISCIPLE'S RESPONSE*

Three

SO, WHAT IS STEWARDSHIP?

Stewardship is the grateful response of a Christian disciple who recognizes and receives God's gifts and shares these gifts generously in love of God and neighbor.

For those of you who may not be familiar with the idea of stewardship, for the record, I must clarify—just in case anyone reading may believe inaccurately or has been taught incorrectly—that stewardship does not mean fundraising. Through what has now been almost three decades, when I travel around the country and ask parishioners what they think stewardship means, this is often the first thing I hear. That stewardship means fundraising. Or money. Unfortunately, neither of these two definitions is an authentic meaning of stewardship.

And, if you are one who believes this stewardship "myth," you are not alone. Even bishops, priests, and seminarians often believe this.

When my husband, Eric, and I visited Rome in May 2013, we were blessed to stay at the North American College. While there, hosted by our lifelong friend and one of the vice-rectors at the time, Fr. Tim McKeown (a sensational tour guide, by the way), we attended the Liturgy of the Hours at the seminary along with multiple daily Masses. After one of the morning Masses, we had a delicious breakfast of blood-red oranges, eggs, and Italian pastries with the seminarians and sat with a charming young man from the Midwest. He kindly asked what Eric and I did for a living, and we responded that we "foster stewardship in Catholic parishes." His eyes lit up, and he said, "Oh, I get it, you are fundraisers!" I sighed. Even future priests have that connotation of stewardship equating to fundraising. That breakfast interaction only made me stick in my heels and desire to promote the true message of stewardship even more loudly.

Let's learn the true meaning.

In *Stewardship: A Disciples Response*, a pastoral letter on stewardship written by the United States Conference of Catholic Bishops, stewardship is described as follows:

"Stewardship is an expression of discipleship, with the power to change how we understand and live out our lives. Disciples who practice stewardship recognize God as the origin of life, the giver of freedom, the source of all they have and are and will be. They are deeply aware of the truth that 'The Lord's are the earth and its fullness; the world and those who dwell in it' (Ps 24:1). They know themselves to be recipients and caretakers of God's many gifts. They are grateful for what they have received and eager to cultivate their gifts out of love for God and one another."

In another section of the pastoral letter, they further describe what identifies a Christian steward:

"As Christian stewards, we receive God's gifts gratefully, cultivate them responsibly, share them lovingly in justice with others, and return them with increase to the Lord."

In addition to these descriptions, the Diocese of Wichita, Kansas—well-known for the roots of Catholic stewardship led by the late stewardship pioneer Msgr. Thomas McGread—created an easy and brief definition of stewardship. To prevent confusion and highlight the most important elements of stewardship, this is what the diocese crafted:

"Stewardship is the grateful response of a Christian disciple who recognizes and receives God's gifts and shares these gifts in love of God and neighbor."

Thus, stewardship is essentially recognizing that everything we have is a gift from God. This includes our material possessions such as our homes, clothes, cars, and food. It encompasses our intelligence and abilities, the talents that make us unique individuals. It includes all of the diverse opportunities we have each day. It also includes our families. It includes our jobs. After all, God gave us the brainpower to qualify for the jobs we hold to earn a living. These freely given gifts even include the very breath we are now breathing. The heart of stewardship is to understand that everything good we have is simply a gift from God. Without Him, we would have nothing.

Moreover, God gifts us everything not because we have earned it or even deserve it. I know I haven't taken any tests to qualify for these blessings. I don't have a certificate that entitles me to them.

Nope, He gives all of it to us simply because He loves us.

And, once we recognize all that we have is a gift from God, we yearn to give back to Him out of gratitude and our need to give. We don't give back to God out of duty, or guilt, or because our pastor or our parents make us. In the Stewardship Way of Life, we always give back in gratitude!

If you are currently parishioners in a parish that promotes the holistic meaning of stewardship, you likely understand stewardship frequently referred to as the Three Ts: Time, Talent, and Treasure.

But, remember, stewardship is not just for parish life.

There is no division: "I'm a steward at Mass or church but not at home, school or work." Wrong! We don't put on our stewardship hats when we walk into church and remove them once we leave. Nope.

Living the life of stewardship is 24/7. It never stops until our very last breath. After all, we never reach a point in our spiritual lives where we can throw in the towel and say that we have reached the pinnacle of discipleship. Can you imagine waking up one day and claiming that you have learned all there is to learn about being a disciple of Jesus Christ? Of course not. There is always more to learn and new ways to grow deeper spiritually.

We are never done growing and living as disciples of Jesus.

"STEWARDSHIP BEGINS
BEFORE WE EVEN STEP
ONTO OUR PARISH
CAMPUSES. IT BEGINS
WITH
our families."

ARE WE STEWARDS AT HOME?

During my time developing stewardship as a way of life in Catholic parishes, I have gleaned quite a collection of statistics. For instance, when I ask parishioners what stewardship means, aside from the initial "money and fundraising" responses, I often hear that it is the time, talent, and treasure lived out in parish life. Parishioners often respond to the question by saying they attend Mass and Adoration, serve as lectors or greeters, or that their children serve as altar servers. They express how they place envelopes in the offertory and are members of a Bible study group. And, although these particular roles are excellent examples of living out stewardship in our parish families, stewardship is so much more.

One of the services we provide our parish clients at Catholic Stewardship Consultants, Inc. (CSC) is to conduct a parish survey every three to five years. One of the questions we include asks parishioners to assess their present understanding of stewardship. This question, and response, showcases how parishioners currently comprehend and live out stewardship. Unfortunately, due to a lack of proper grasp, many parishioners see stewardship as only a "parish thing." When asked to define stewardship in their own words, respondents exclaim things such as "stewardship is about sharing my time, talents and money with our parish" or "stewardship is about giving money to my church" or "stewardship is volunteering at my parish."

Rarely do I ever hear someone share that stewardship applies before you arrive or once you leave the parish campus.

Another service we provide to the parishes we work with is a custom, digital parish newsletter. This platform is not a "one size fits all" approach. Instead, we believe it's essential to communicate, educate and evangelize with parish families so that they are aware of what is at the heart of their beloved parish home. Of course, ongoing Catholic faith formation is critical, but it's also essential for the communication to be about the parish they call home. These custom newsletters help parishioners best understand what opportunities are available to them, to learn how being involved has spiritually impacted their fellow parishioners, and how they can grow as disciples through ongoing formation. In short, showcasing what is available to them within the walls of their parish home and how being involved can deepen their faith.

Recently, one of the writers on our staff interviewed a parishioner for an article about a particular parish ministry.

When the writer contacted the interviewee, the man immediately apologized for his recent inability to be as involved as he initially planned to be when he joined this ministry. He planned to attend most of the ministry events and meetings and hoped to be more hands-on. But he had been so busy taking care of his father (who had been suffering from terminal cancer) that he wasn't able to be as involved as he initially hoped.

You will never believe what he said next.

He said now that his father has passed away, he will have more free time to be a good steward.

Hearing this broke my heart.

Now I don't know about you, but there may not be a better example of sharing your time, talent, and treasure as a steward than helping someone on death's doorstep. However, this man believed he was being a "bad" steward since he wasn't doing it in a parish setting.

This is a perfect example of the misunderstanding of stewardship and how much it weaves into every facet of our lives.

Stewardship is meant to be lived everywhere. You only need to view it through the proper lens.

I recently had a doctor's appointment at a local retina center. The median age of patients there is 85. I was awestruck by the loving caregivers—sons and daughters, even grandchildren—who were taking their loved ones to seek medical help. Some pushed wheelchairs. Others filled out paperwork. Still, others were just present so their relative or friend wouldn't be alone. These people were sharing the gift of their time to care for another person.

Stewardship is not just about going to Mass once a week and being in the choir. It's not just about helping with Vacation Bible School or the parish picnic. It isn't just about giving financially to the parish. Of course, those are all essential parts of stewardship, yes.

Let's remember that stewardship begins before we even step onto our parish campuses. It begins with our families.

"THE FAMILY IS
THE MOST ANCIENT
INSTITUTION WHICH
GOD FOUNDED IN
PARADISE WHEN HE
CALLED THE FIRST PAIR
OF HUMAN BEINGS INTO
EXISTENCE. THE FIRST
BLESSING WHICH GOD
GAVE WAS FOR THE
wellbeing
OF THE FAMILY."

— SAINT JOHN VIANNEY

Five

WHAT IS A DOMESTIC CHURCH?

According to Saint John Vianney, "The family is the most ancient institution which God founded in paradise when He called the first pair of human beings into existence. The first blessing which God gave was for the wellbeing of the family."

We all know what a family is. You may have also heard the phrase "Domestic Church." But do you know what a "Domestic Church" is?

The term "Domestic Church" simply refers to the family, the smallest body of gathered believers in Christ. The term dates back to the first century A.D. and means "little church." Our early Church fathers understood the home was fertile ground for discipleship, sanctification, and holiness.

The domestic church plays a key role in our holiness because it is the primary place where we practice coming to intimately love other persons. It allows our families the opportunity to honor God, respect His laws, and pray together regularly in our homes where virtues must be regularly demonstrated through our words and actions.

The emphasis that our recent popes, especially Saint Pope John Paul II, Pope Benedict, and Pope Francis have placed on the family speaks to the profound dignity and importance of our domestic churches.

Here is a pertinent reminder of the purposes of our "little churches" from Pope Francis:

"Love is shown by little things, by attention to small daily signs which make us feel at home. Faith grows when it is lived and shaped by love. That is why our families, our homes, are true domestic churches."

DOMESTIC FORMATION IS NEEDED NOW MORE THAN EVER

One thing that 2020 taught the Catholic Church is how truly vital our domestic churches are. With the global pandemic, its quarantines, and the subsequent closings of our beloved parish homes, growing and living out our Catholic faith from home became more critical than ever before.

For example, in April 2020, many Catholics experienced our first "at-home" Triduum, Easter, and Pentecost. We were forced to experience the most extraordinary liturgical seasons of our Catholic faith sidelined at home. For most of us, it was surreal. How did we respond? Did our domestic churches "skip" these key seasons since we couldn't fully celebrate under our parish roofs? Or did we dig deep, be as creative as possible, and find a way to share these sacred times with our family members at home despite the shutdown?

During this religious "drought" many of us utilized online resources to enhance our spiritual lives. Whether it was livestreaming Mass, participating in virtual Rosaries or Bible studies, or partaking of Bishop Barron's *Word on Fire, FORMED, Ascension Presents,* or *Blessed is She,* online opportunities allowed us to continue our family's faith formation at a time when we could not be physically present. As we resume normalcy after the pandemic, our domestic churches can continue to incorporate the best of these online resources into family life. These online options, combined with our traditional in-person faith practices, will only help our domestic churches flourish.

"AS THE FAMILY
GOES, SO GOES
the nation
AND THE WHOLE
WORLD."

— SAINT POPE JOHN PAUL II

Six

WHAT IS YOUR FAMILY MISSION?

Today it seems that every business, school, social club, and charitable organization has a mission statement. These statements express the purpose and goals of the particular entity. Often, we see these mission statements prominently placed at the entrance of the building, on websites, and listed on printed promotional materials.

So, what about our families? Should they have a mission statement too?

After all, our families are much dearer to us than any business or organization could ever be. We want the members of our family to thrive and excel in life, and as parents and grandparents, we want to ensure we provide a nurturing, enriching, and encouraging environment. Clarifying what we, as a family, want, need, and strive for can help cultivate a clear roadmap for all family members to answer the Call to Holiness.

In 1981, Saint Pope John Paul II crafted the Apostolic Exhortation titled *Familiaris Consortio (The Fellowship of the Family)*. This in-depth letter refers to marriage as one of the most precious and most urgent tasks of Christian couples in our time. Rightly so, especially when society has only continued through the last few decades to minimize the importance of the nuclear family.

In part three of the letter, when Saint Pope John Paul II touches on "The Role of the Christian Family" he states: "The family finds in the plan of God the Creator and Redeemer not only its identity, what it is, but also its mission, what it can and should do. The role that God calls the family to perform in history derives from what the family is; its role represents the dynamic and existential development of what it is. Each family finds within itself a summons that cannot be ignored, and that specifies both its dignity and its responsibility: family, become what you are" (CF 17).

His urge for our families to become what we are is a cry for all of us to respond to the Call to Holiness on the family level. Considering what your summons as a family is and allowing your family to become what God intended is a critical step in fostering ongoing family discipleship.

Saint Pope John Paul II goes on to say: "All members of the family, each according to his or her own gift, have the grace and responsibility of building, day by day, the communion of persons, making the family 'a school of deeper humanity': this happens where there is care and love for the little ones, the sick, the aged; where there is mutual service every day; when there is a sharing of goods, of joys and of sorrows" (CF 21).

Family life is chock full of opportunities to share our God-given gifts. We see this as parents and grandparents care for little ones, as family members tend to one another in sickness and as children care for their aging parents and grandparents. This mutual sharing of both triumphs and tribulations is what seals families.

Having a family mission statement, even one not formally written down like a business plan, helps us articulate how our unique family lives out stewardship. Taking the time and effort to create a mission statement is a means of "stewarding" our own family. Consider the values and virtues of discipleship that are most significant to your loved ones and incorporate them into the statement to answer, "What is your family's sacred purpose?"

The family mission statement doesn't have to be complicated. Keeping it simple will allow you to execute it more easily. Think of the little tweaks you could make to enhance the mission of discipleship within your family.

If your mission is rooted in God's plan, you cannot fail.

"SET OUT FOR THE
GREAT CITY OF
NINEVEH, AND PREACH
AGAINST IT; FOR
THEIR WICKEDNESS
HAS COME BEFORE
ME. BUT JONAH MADE
READY TO FLEE
TO TARSHISH,
away from
THE LORD."

— JONAH 1:2-3

Seven

ARE YOU RUNNING FROM A "WHALE" OF A MISSION?

A s you are assessing what your family mission is and how God is calling you to grow in holiness, consider if you are avoiding a particular tug at your heart.

Sometimes God calls our families to tasks and roles we don't feel qualified for or capable of completing. We may think that other families are better suited for the task at hand. However, when we receive a special nudge from the Holy Spirit, typically, it is a customized calling that only our families can finish. If we don't respond, the call goes unanswered and unfulfilled.

I attended a women's retreat a few years ago, and the theme was "What Is Your Nineveh?" I had never considered that before. To be honest, I never really took the time to fully understand how the prophet Jonah responded to God's calling for him. I loved learning more about his story. Instead of responding to the Lord's prompting,

Jonah decided to run in the opposite direction. Where did that get him? To safety? To peace? Absolutely not! Jonah landed in the belly of a whale. And, when the whale spits out Jonah, he landed exactly where the Lord wanted him in the first place.

Life is funny like that.

The retreat leader asked us if the Lord had asked us, or our families, to answer a particular calling. And if instead of answering, we chose to run in the other direction like Jonah. Once I took time to pray about it, I realized that there are moments in my past when the Holy Spirit had gently nudged me to accomplish something that I didn't feel prepared or qualified to do. Immediately, I responded with a "no," running in the other direction of the request. How easily did I think, "There is no way I (or my family) could accomplish such a difficult ask—Not me! Not us!" And, then after I paused and refused the request again, I felt that tapping again on my heart. God is persistent if we only take a pause and listen to His encouragement.

The speaker emboldened us to not run like Jonah did—in the complete opposite direction. She also pointed out that Jonah also did only the bare minimum once he arrived in Nineveh. As a prophet, he lacked depth or conviction. As stewards, when God taps on our hearts, we need to do the opposite of Jonah. We need to be mindful to act to the best of our abilities—to share our talents—and not just respond with a disinterested and unfocused heart. We shouldn't think, "What is the least I need to do?" Instead, we should ask ourselves, "How can I fully fulfill God's call to share my gifts with others?"

When our daughter Ashlin was a junior in our local diocesan

Catholic high school, her literature teacher reached out to me. There was an upcoming Georgia Right to Life speech contest, and she thought Ashlin should participate. I was honestly surprised because, since Ashlin was a middle child, she wasn't enthusiastic about public speaking. I was right. When proposed, Ashlin politely declined. However, after a bit of extra encouragement from her teacher and also from Eric and me, prompting her to use her gifts, she apprehensively agreed. The evening of the contest, I decided not to record her presentation. After all, I didn't want to distract her or make her extra nervous. So, I sat quietly in a chair in the back. I said a quick prayer before she started thinking she may be anxious.

Was I wrong!

From the first word she uttered, the entire room was captivated. You could hear a pin drop. She spoke eloquently with authority and conviction. She gracefully shared her presentation titled "We Are the Pro-Life Generation" with the panel of judges and those in the audience, and by the end, I had tears in my eyes. Ashlin gave it her all, won that contest that evening, and came home with the $200 prize money. Her teacher saw something in Ashlin and encouraged her to share it with others. Even though she was apprehensive at first, Ashlin took a leap of faith, and God was there to meet her.

Ashlin demonstrated how we should listen and respond confidently to where God is calling us and our families to use our talents even if we don't feel qualified for the task (or want to initially run in the opposite direction, like Jonah). God will provide the grace to get the job done. The key is to not rely on ourselves alone; instead, we need to rely on our talents and His grace.

Furthermore, we must remember that others need our gifts, and stewardship allows us to share these God-given abilities with others. Don't dismiss a call—it may seem challenging; however, remember that with God, nothing is impossible.

"LOVE IS SHOWN BY LITTLE
THINGS, BY ATTENTION
TO SMALL DAILY SIGNS
WHICH MAKE US FEEL
AT HOME. FAITH GROWS
WHEN IT IS LIVED AND
SHAPED BY LOVE. THAT
IS WHY OUR FAMILIES,

our homes,

ARE TRUE DOMESTIC
CHURCHES."

— POPE FRANCIS

Eight

HOME SWEET (STEWARDSHIP) HOME

If you're fully embracing stewardship as a way of life, your "Domestic Church" should look a little different.

Let's face it, not all of our homes look like the ones featured on HGTV. You know what I am talking about—perfectly positioned furniture and decorations that scream of the latest interior and exterior trends. And honestly, our homes shouldn't. After all, most of us have children (and pets) that fill them with all of the belongings and chaos that accompanies such a life.

However, aside from how tidy or messy your home is or how updated or outdated your home is, there is one thing that should be present inside: A witness of your faith! Would someone entering your home know that you are a Christian? A Catholic? What is inside your house that would let others know you serve God?

A LITTLE GOLF TOURNAMENT

Our family lives in Augusta, Georgia. If you are a golf fan (and even if you are not) you may have heard of a little golf tournament that the Augusta National hosts each year during the first week of April. Maybe the words "The Masters" ring a bell? This golf tournament brings thousands of people to our town each Spring— golfers, caddies, coaches, family members, spectators, journalists, caterers, and countless numbers of service providers.

It's a golf haven! The world comes to Augusta that week.

For us locals, it is a bit of an Augusta tradition to rent out our homes to these golf-loving fans, players, and coaches. After all, the local hotels get booked solid, and renting a home allows for much more space to sprawl out than a small hotel space.

The beauty is if you rent your home out during Masters Week, the money earned is 100-percent tax-free.

Yep, you read correctly.

So, you can bet when my husband, Eric, and I got married, we wanted to jump on that bandwagon as soon as we became homeowners.

Once we did, I called a few of the rental agencies and asked them to come to tour our home to see if it could be considered rentable. To ensure the space looked its best, I cleaned it from top to bottom to make it sparkle for its debut. The representatives from the agency arrived and I welcomed them into our home for a walk-through. They were warm and kind and traipsed from room to room to survey the potential rental space.

Following them around, I heard a bit of quiet chatter. Something along the lines of "Wow, I think they have a crucifix hanging in each room of this home."

I froze.

I immediately wondered if I was going to have to remove my religious articles from the walls of our home in order to rent it. For a nanosecond, that is.

Then, I regained my senses and realized that if renters wanted to rent our home, the crucifixes (and the other sacramentals inside) would stay exactly as is.

Do you know what?

We have rented our "crucifix-filled" home for the last 20 years to all kinds of golf fans, players, coaches, caddies, and service providers.

I never removed one Christian-oriented item and, to top it off, each year I leave out a list of Holy Thursday, Good Friday, and Easter Sunday Mass schedules from our local Catholic parish as the tournament week often falls during the Triduum.

I can't tell you how many notes I have received through the years from our renters. Some compliment a wall paint color or thank us for letting them use our home. Several notes have specifically thanked us for inviting them to worship at our local parish during such an important liturgical time. The renters stated that being able to attend the Triduum services and Easter Mass while away from home was extra special.

You never know who your house will speak to and what it will convey.

FAITH IN UNCERTAIN TIMES

Aside from the one week each year when we rent our home to avid golf aficionados, our family enjoys and lives out the day-to-day drills in our home. It's filled with countless memories of joys, heartaches, and laughter and I cherish every one of them. I am sure the same is true for your home.

When COVID-19 struck and the quarantine hit, times were especially challenging for all of us. On top of the "normal" challenging moments in life, most of us were knocked to our knees from fear of the virus, the potential change in livelihood, and the stressors ranging from locating toilet paper to schooling our children at home to watching our loved ones perish in a hospital room that none of us could even visit.

These times of tribulation, when things appear bleak and dark, are times where living our faith at home is especially essential.

Having sacramentals in our homes allows us to turn to the strength of our faith when times are tough. These objects remind us that we are not alone, and Christ is always with us. Helping us get through tragedy and anxiety and even normal disappointments are all made easier through that domestic faith connection, especially when we can't get to our physical church buildings.

That was the case for all of us in 2020.

BLESSINGS AND BREAKING BREAD

Do you have your homes blessed by your priest or deacon? If not, why? There is no better way to spiritually seal your home as a pillar of your faith! Plus, it is a great way to get to know the spiritual shepherd of your flock with the bonus of sharing a coffee, meal, or dessert.

We have had each of the houses in which we have lived blessed by our pastor or Eric's father, who is a deacon. And, we have had it done periodically after that first blessing. I know I always feel a great sense of comfort and peace once our home has been blessed knowing that God is with us every step of our day.

Don't just stop at the ordained members of the parish. Think of the families you see every week (or used to see) at Mass. The ones that sit in the same pew every week and smile and nod at you as they arrive and depart. Do you even know their names? Have you ever invited those fellow parishioners over to your home for a barbecue or a cup of coffee? These invitations allow your home to be filled with your parish family and help to provide a personal connection that extends beyond the walls of the church building.

COFFEE TABLE MEMORIES

A few years ago, during Masters Week, when we were renting out our home, we were blessed to share the week in Hilton Head Island, South Carolina, with one of our close priest friends, Fr. Jim Golka (now Bishop Jim Golka of the Diocese of Colorado Springs, Colorado). Fr. Jim is warm-hearted and comes from a big family, so he is naturally great with kids.

At that particular time, our youngest daughter, Ava, was preparing to receive her First Holy Communion in just a few short weeks. She was a bit confused about the whole "magic" that happens on the altar (the words of an 8-year-old, not mine!) When Fr. Jim heard her confusion, he was happy to explain transubstantiation—which as a six-syllable word is not in the typical vocabulary list for a second-grader.

He cleared the coffee table in the living room and grabbed a few decorative objects nearby to improv as he walked Ava through the words and meanings of what happens on the altar as the "bread and wine" become the "body and blood" of Christ. Ava's eyes were huge in wonder as she hung on every word of his explanation. Forever, she will have that memory from Fr. Jim chiseled in her heart. To this day, it is one of the fondest memories I have of her First Holy Communion.

VACATIONING WITH VOCATIONS

As you may imagine, priests are living their best lives—with jam-packed schedules, that is. Shepherding their flocks, now often in clusters of more than one parish, celebrating Masses, administering sacraments, counseling those in need, along with attending countless meetings and planning for the spiritual future of their parishes... the list is long and can even be lonely. No doubt our spiritual fathers need some rest and relaxation. So, if you are in a position to include your pastor on a short getaway—with you or even solo to one of your favorite vacation places for a small retreat—do it!

When our oldest daughter, Alanna, was involved in Irish dancing, she qualified to dance at the North American Nationals that were held in Ontario, Canada, in July 2008. Our pastor at the time, Fr. Jerry Ragan, loved to travel and this part of Canada was on his bucket list at a time when he could actually accompany us. Plus, a few fellow parishioners were attending the competition so he could cheer on Alanna and some of her fellow dancers who were also members of our parish. It was a fantastic trip of dancing and fellowship and making family memories with one of God's finest.

I recall other trips spent on the sandy beaches of Tybee Island, Georgia, with two other priest friends of ours, Fr. John Lyons and Msgr. James Costigan. A family tradition for over a decade, we enjoyed Lowcountry boils, beach walks, boat rides with dolphins and Mass at the tiny island church of Saint Michael. On one specific trip, we were unpacking our bags in an old convent that had been converted into a house when our middle daughter, Ashlin, who was around 4 at the time, opened the refrigerator hoping to find a snack after our three-hour car ride. Instead of finding juice or a treat, she found something unexpected. She yelled in her loudest toddler voice, "Mom, Jesus is in the refrigerator!"

Surprised, Eric and I ran into the kitchen wondering what in the world she was talking about.

When we opened the fridge door, there were unconsecrated hosts packaged in the refrigerator. They were being stored in there since the house was often used by diocesan priests for a place to stay while visiting the beach. To 4-year-old Ashlin, she knew those circular-shaped pieces of bread in the fridge were clearly what the priest consecrated on the altar to become Jesus' real flesh. To her, those were Jesus. It warmed my heart that she made that connection at that young age and yelled it out with such joy.

You never know where and when your family faith life will unfold. Even when your family unit is outside of your home—on vacation or running errands or visiting family and friends—living out our call to stewardship continues. Our domestic churches—all diverse and packed with miles of unique memories—expand as we celebrate our beliefs and Church teachings wherever we are. Each moment (and location) is yet another opportunity to live out the Call to Holiness.

"THE MOST
EXTRAORDINARY
THING IN THE WORLD
IS AN ORDINARY MAN
AND AN ORDINARY
WOMAN AND THEIR

ordinary

CHILDREN."

— G.K. CHESTERTON

Nine

ALL SHAPES
AND SIZES

Families come in all shapes and sizes.

There is no perfect family—God made us all unique and special. Some of us have big families, some of us have small families. Some of us are single, some married, some divorced, some widowed. Some come from a traditional, nuclear family and some of us come from a dysfunctional, hot mess. The combinations are endless and yet there are so many diverse and beautiful examples of family.

Additionally, each of our families has a special stewardship story that only you and your family can live out. It is unique to you, much like a fingerprint.

What does your family look like?

I married my college sweetheart. My best friend (also named Lisa) introduced me to Eric at a bar under the guise that my mother would like him because "he was Catholic and from a big Catholic family." At that point, I had never dated a Catholic, and my mom was fervently praying (and expressing) that there had to be a nice Catholic boy out there somewhere to date. So, Lisa introduced us and, well, the rest is history. We were engaged after six months and married eight months later—one short week after I graduated from college. Eric and I have five daughters ranging in age from 11 to 25, which means we have an elementary school child, a middle school child, and a college student along with two other adult children as well—one who is married and who has blessed us with our first son-in-law and two grandchildren. So, we have recently earned our new roles as not only mother-in-law and father-in-law but also Mimi and PapPap and couldn't be more thrilled.

I was raised by parents who are both children of Midwestern farmers, and we moved frequently, as my dad is a contract mechanical engineer. My mom graciously stayed on the homefront to raise me and my younger sister and by the time I was in middle school I had seen much of the country already. Cradle Catholics who have been married for over 50 years, my parents are hardworking, loving, and devout, and service is their love language. If you even mention you need help with anything, they will appear before you can blink. Both my sister and I gave them the surprise of their adult lives as we each have five children giving them a whopping 10 grandbabies to love.

Eric, on the other hand, is the oldest of nine children, raised by his father, who is a CPA, a deacon in the Catholic Church, and his mother who is a (now-retired) pediatric physical therapist. Cradle Catholics—a ballerina and model and a motorcycle-riding weightlifter—who married shortly after college and recently celebrated their 52nd wedding anniversary. Moreover, Eric and his eight siblings have blessed his parents with a total of 34 grandchildren and two great-grandchildren.

We are blessed to share the gift of faith and family with all but one of our siblings living in our same town. This means that birthdays, sacraments, holidays, and school and extracurricular events are regularly shared by all of us locals. Family birthday parties and holidays boast an attendance of 50-plus, and that is what is normal to us. When I was growing up, that would have been an unthinkable crowd to me. When I was little if more than four people sat at our kitchen table it was crowded!

You never know the plan God will unfold for your family life. Remember, He is not done as family life ever evolves day by day.

Saint Thomas More said this of family and I couldn't agree more: "Family life is full of major and minor crises—the ups and downs of health, success and failure in career, marriage, and divorce—and all kinds of characters. It is tied to places and events and histories. With all of these felt details, life etches itself into memory and personality. It's difficult to imagine anything more nourishing to the soul."

Amazingly, Saint Thomas More lived between 1438 and 1535 and shared these sentiments during that period. Even today his words still ring true.

Part 1 Summary

EXPLORE AND UNPACK
STEWARDSHIP

If you've never stopped to consider the true definition of stewardship, take some time to ponder its meaning for you and your family. Remember it is not just meant for parish life. Living out stewardship in our families is worth exploring and unpacking. This is also where we daily live out our lives as Christ's disciples.

The same is true about the Call to Holiness. This call isn't just intended for those specific ordained leaders or the saints. If, in the past, you feel like you could never share a path with such inspirational persons, why not start envisioning yourself walking beside them step by step?

After all, you would be in some great company.

Living the life of stewardship can seem intimidating at first. The idea of letting go and letting God's Will direct our lives can be tough for most of us, especially we control freaks. Yet, letting loose on our grip and instead being open to God's plan for our families can be richly rewarding.

Bishop Barron touches on this concept and refers to it as the "Loop of Grace." He says: "It all begins with grace, and it all ends with grace. Bernanos' country priest summed up Christianity with the phrase, '*Toute est grace*,' which means, 'Everything is grace.' God gives graciously, gratuitously, superabundantly—and then we are called to respond with a similar exuberance. The more we give back to God, the more we get, and then we must give that back again, so as to get even more in return. This is the loop of grace which is spoken of from beginning to end of the Bible."

"FAMILY LIFE IS FULL OF MAJOR AND MINOR CRISES—THE UPS AND DOWNS OF HEALTH, SUCCESS AND FAILURE IN CAREER, MARRIAGE, AND DIVORCE—AND ALL KINDS OF CHARACTERS. IT IS TIED TO PLACES AND EVENTS AND HISTORIES. WITH ALL OF THESE FELT DETAILS, LIFE ETCHES ITSELF INTO MEMORY AND PERSONALITY. IT'S DIFFICULT TO IMAGINE ANYTHING *more nourishing* TO THE SOUL."

— SAINT THOMAS MORE

Part 2

LIVING AS A STEWARDSHIP FAMILY: THE THREE Ts OF FAMILY LIFE

By this point, I hope it is apparent that stewardship is not just meant for our parishes. Remember, when we embrace Stewardship as a Way of Life it permeates into all areas of our lives—wherever we are!

Next, let's look at how our families live out the Three Ts of Stewardship: Time, Talent, and Treasure.

Likely, you are already doing these stewardship scenarios and you may not even realize it. If so, great work. If not, maybe they will inspire you to commit to one or more of them as a family. No matter where we currently stand in our faith journeys, God is always calling us to grow closer to Him. We are never done learning and stretching as disciples.

Let's start with Time.

"KNOW THAT EVEN
WHEN YOU ARE IN THE
KITCHEN, OUR LORD

moves amidst

THE POTS AND PANS."

———

— SAINT TERESA OF AVILA

Ten

STEWARDSHIP OF TIME
HOLINESS IS FOR ALL HOME LIFE

Whether you are single and looking for your vocation, newly married and adapting to life with a spouse, have a new baby or 10 children, dealing with tweens or teenagers, launching young adults off to college or careers, welcoming new in-laws as your children wed, becoming grandparents, enjoying retirement, or facing being a widow, stewardship applies to all seasons of life.

Before Eric and I got married, I felt like I was an "above average" Catholic. I went to Mass and sometimes even daily Mass. I went to Confession regularly. I kept the Commandments. Check. Check. Check. When I was single, I felt like a good Catholic when I followed these Catholic "rules." It seemed effortless.

Then we had a baby.

Now completing my checklist was not so easy. Whenever I wanted to go to Mass, it seemed like the baby was too fussy. If I tried to go to my Adoration hour, it was during her naptime. All of a sudden, my normal traditions of living out my faith no longer worked. Ugh.

I was frustrated that I couldn't complete my checklist and I got upset I couldn't be an "above average" Catholic anymore. I didn't know how to function in this new season and was ready to give up.

Worse yet, I realized my Catholic "checklist" was a horrible indicator of me being a solid Catholic.

So, I learned new ways.

Thankfully, my wise mother-in-law (remember she has nine children) imparted some wisdom to my "newbie" mom self.

She gave me a book, one of her golden oldies, called *Holiness for Housewives* by Hubert Van Zeller. Then, she told me to stop praying like a single woman now that I was a married woman with a child. Smart plan.

I didn't realize that I needed to stretch and bend and be flexible in my new life season. Her encouragement allowed me to slightly alter the ways that I fulfilled my faith obligations. Eric and I alternated Mass times on the Sundays the baby was fussy. I asked my mom or sister to keep the baby so I could pop into the Adoration chapel when I wanted to pray in a more peaceful setting. More importantly, I found new ways to pray—while nursing the baby or while rocking her to sleep. Even when I was in the kitchen tackling domestic duties, I would talk to God.

And, you know what... it worked.

I simply needed to adapt to the new season of life I was entering. It took a bit of time to get it right, but remaining open and flexible helped. So did giving myself some grace along the way.

Since then, I have entered many new seasons. Some have been more challenging than others. Nevertheless, if I pause and take some time to consider ways to tweak my faith life, I can always find a way to move forward. It may not look like I anticipated, but God always surprises me with His creative methods.

"IT'S NOT ENOUGH TO BE
BUSY, SO ARE THE ANTS. THE
QUESTION IS, WHAT ARE WE
busy about?"

— HENRY DAVID THOREAU

PUTTING YOUR FAMILY FIRST:

Stewardship Families Make Intentional Commitments

I am a "yes" girl. You know the kind—I immediately say "yes" to almost any question without taking much time to consider the consequences. Do you need me to be room mom? Sure. Do you need me to watch your dog? Of course. Do you need me to cut out 100 triangles for the kindergartners? Not a problem.

Part of the reason I am inclined to nod at requests is I am a people pleaser and I want to help. The other part of my quick agreement is because I feel guilty saying "no." After all, aren't we supposed to help others when they ask us?

For years, my husband, Eric, would ask me to better discern what commitments I was making, but I typically ignored Eric's promptings as I wanted to remain "charitable."

Early on, my interpretation of charitable was a bit skewed.

Let me explain.

Come with me back to December 17, 2010. A week before Christmas. You know the drill—it's an extremely busy time of year for everyone. For me, the mama of five kiddos the night before the last day of school before Christmas break meant my "yes list" was super long! That evening I had teachers' gift baskets to assemble, coaches' cookies to bake, Christmas cards to fill out, preschool presents to organize, office staff gifts to wrap... you get the gist.

That particular night we had our good friend, Fr. Ben Dallas, over for dinner. Fr. Ben is witty and a superb storyteller, so it's always a treat to share a meal and fellowship with him. He and Eric were chatting after we finished dessert and I was zooming around trying to get the girls ready for bed. The older girls were studying for their finals, and I finally got the middle two girls to sleep. The only one left to put to bed was the baby.

Determined, I gently rocked her to sleep and as I was walking up to her nursery, I was extra quiet in hopes she would easily settle into her crib. When I laid her down, she did relax every muscle and sink sweetly into slumber. I was grateful and tiptoed out of the nursery ensuring that I didn't make a squeak. I even took off my shoes and only wore socks so she couldn't hear my footsteps. Once the nursery door was quietly shut, I turned and scurried down the stairs... in my socks.

Did I mention our stairs are hardwood?

I started at the top of the staircase and stayed in mid-air until I reached the landing, 12 steps later. With a loud thud, I hit the wood landing and all inside could hear the "crack" that rattled throughout the house.

My humerus broke completely in half.

Eric came running up to see what happened. The older girls

who were studying ran from their schoolwork to check on me, and the little girls awoke after hearing my screams. And, of course, the baby started crying from her crib.

As I lay at the bottom of the stairs in writhing pain, arm throbbing but also in a state of shock, do you know what I was thinking?

I'll give you some hints. It was not the concern for my arm or what the next steps would be. Nope. It wasn't the plan for containing the ever-increasing pain level. Nada. It wasn't anxiety over a potential surgery to fix the second largest bone in my body. No.

I was upset that I would not be able to tackle those items on the "to do" list tonight.

Talk about wrong ordering priorities!

Not being intentional about what I said "yes" to caused me to take my eye off the ball. Time and time again, I found myself constantly distracted with what I had to do for those outside our home instead of what I needed to do for those inside of my home—for my own immediate crew, including myself.

During my long one-year road to recovery—after having a metal rod added to my skeleton during surgery, almost a year of painful physical therapy, and having to hire a sweet nanny to help me with the five kiddos, especially the baby—I realized I had it all backward.

Of course, we are supposed to be charitable. We are called to help those in need. We are to step up when available to aid others. What we are not supposed to do is put those choices in front of our vocation. The vocation we receive from God.

When I tried to do too much for others, I forgot my primary call.

It took a huge wake-up call for me to, well, wake up.

Remember, saying "no" to something else intentionally is saying "yes" to something for your family. Stop trying to "busy" yourself to death.

Fr. Gary Kastl, a close friend and a stellar retreat leader in his own right, regularly states in his presentation at our stewardship conferences that "being busy is not the same thing as being vibrant." I couldn't agree more.

"BE STILL AND
KNOW THAT I AM
God."

— PSALM 46:11

STOP ENDLESSLY DOING:

STEWARDSHIP FAMILIES "JUST BE"

Are you too busy for your family?

One of my favorite dynamic young priests—Fr. Brian O'Brien, who is the pastor at a vibrant stewardship parish in Stillwater, Oklahoma—once said on his entertaining podcast, "Pastors of Payne," that we are Human Beings, NOT Human Doings.

Take that in for a moment.

In order to hear God's soft, gentle call in our life we have to be still long enough to listen. When do you pause long enough in your day to hear God's voice?

These days it feels odd to not have a phone in our hand, our computers buzzing, or Netflix streaming. That is on top of the normal advertisements we see on our screens, on billboards, and aired on Spotify or the radio. People are wearing noise-canceling earbuds and headphones in an attempt to lessen the noise around us.

And, let's face it, we are frequently uncomfortable being still. After all, if there are no distractions and no noise, we may actually have to face some of our concerns, worries, or fears. Maybe the distractions are desired so that we don't have to face the tough stuff.

However, if we want to really connect with God—and His call for our lives—we must carve opportunities to listen.

Even if you can't frequent Adoration or drop by the church, you can intentionally find a way to stop "doing" and just "be." Even if that space is in your closet hiding for a bit from the rest of the family. (No judgment here!) Don't be afraid to seek these opportunities. Often, it is in these quiet encounters that the Holy Spirit will move us and guide us to where God is calling.

A few years ago, Eric traveled to Lexington, Kentucky, and hoped to hit confession before his evening meeting. The rector of the cathedral he was visiting kindly obliged. Eric was a bit surprised at his penance but happily fulfilled it.

Do you want in on what it was?

He was to put away his cell phone and computer and tablet and go to the nearby Arboretum State Botanical Garden of Kentucky to just rest in nature for an hour. He was to not think about anything else but just be still with God and His creation. After packing up his tech gear, Eric headed to the gardens and basked in the serene beauty of God's creations. He told me later that it was the most rejuvenating hour he had experienced in years. Years. I have to admit I was a tad jealous of his penance.

Why do we not give ourselves permission to pause, to ponder, and to press reset? As stewards, we must aim to practice the lost art of being, of listening, and of "not doing." Remember we hear God's call not with our ears, but within our hearts. Open them to God!

"THE FAMILY
THAT PRAYS
together
STAYS
TOGETHER."

PRAYER CONNECTIONS WITH FAMILY:

STEWARDSHIP FAMILIES PRAY TOGETHER DAILY

In my work with parishes around the country, I have also derived much about the "ins and outs" of family prayer time from the thousands of parish surveys we have conducted. For instance, I regularly find that families pray together at Mass and say grace before meals. Although this is a great start, it is also usually the end of family prayer time for most practicing Catholic families. What we have learned, time and time again, in active Catholic families, is that spouses rarely pray together as a couple. Additionally, we find that parents don't regularly pray with their children. On average it is under 20 percent.

If you do not currently pray with your spouse, I encourage you to take a step to do so. Pray for your marriage, for your children, for your in-laws, etc. As a team, be united in prayer. It may seem awkward at first, and that is okay. Start small. Say one *Our Father* together. Then, add some intentions. Before long you will be comfortable and even find solace in this special time together praying for those you love.

Praying with kids and grandkids is also a great opportunity to teach and train young disciples and help form a daily habit. After all, what an excellent example to emulate as they grow up and even when they form their own future domestic churches. Again, this doesn't have to be rocket science. Briefly have each family member pray for an intention and then say an *Our Father*, *Hail Mary*, and a *Glory Be* before lights out is a simple way to set an evening prayer habit.

Often, setting a prayer habit when the kids are young can make this process easier. If the children are raised with daily prayers—whether that is a cross on their forehead before they leave the house in the morning, praise and worship music in the car, grace before meals, or nighttime prayers before bed—it will be an expected part of their routine. Even if they drop the routine when they leave for college, begin their career, or leave the "nest," it will be part of their prayer DNA.

In our home around 8:30 or 9:00 p.m., we say intentions from the evening prayer from the "Liturgy of the Hours." I had never prayed these prayers before I met Eric and his family. His dad is a deacon and, as a member of the clergy, he is required to say the Divine Office (or Liturgy of the Hours) daily. So, this type of prayer habit is what Eric grew up with. When we married, he wanted to continue doing it with our family, and I agreed.

If you are in our house at that hour, passing through to borrow a cup of sugar, or visiting with one of our kiddos, you will be invited to join us in the living room for prayers. Yep. Many visitors who have not likely prayed with their families out loud for years (or maybe ever) pray with us. Classmates pray with us. Neighbors pray with us.

Boyfriends pray with us. Priests even pray with us. Whoever is in our home at that time joins in, and during intentions, they pray for their families and needs. Sometimes, they blush because they don't know how to do it, but mostly they seem excited to pray for their loved ones. It is one of my favorite prayer memories with our family.

After prayers, we take time to get the kids settled before they hit the sack. We find that during those quiet, after-prayer moments we learn the most about how the kids are doing. Often, in the afternoon after school is dismissed, children don't say too much when you ask, "How was school?" Usually, the response is simply "It was fine." However, I find that in the darkened silence of their room after prayer time, they open up because they know you are focused and listening without distractions. So, after prayers, we have some one-on-one time to really learn about their day—what they're excited about or worried about. It's amazing what Eric and I learn during that time. All the secrets come gushing out.

Every family has a unique schedule and style, so there are tons of different options for incorporating prayers into the rhythm of your days. Find one that works for your family, and you won't regret it.

"IT IS NOT
TECHNOLOGY
THAT DETERMINES
WHETHER OR NOT
COMMUNICATION
IS AUTHENTIC, BUT
RATHER THE HUMAN
HEART AND OUR
CAPACITY TO
use wisely
THE MEANS
AT OUR DISPOSAL."

— POPE FRANCIS

SOCIAL DISTRACTIONS:

STEWARDSHIP FAMILIES ARE PRESENT TO ONE ANOTHER

I cannot speak about time without touching on the area of social media.

When we think of technology, we frequently think of the teens and tweens who are fully embracing the latest tech trends. However, let's face it. Social distractions are not just for the younger generations.

If you are out in public, take a moment to observe those around you. Whether you are at a mall, a restaurant, a baseball game, the doctor's office, or a meeting you will likely find that everyone is holding their phone, tablet, or computer.

It's the hardest for me to watch this common scenario at restaurants. Sitting at a table where the kids are staring at a movie on an iPad while the parents are mindlessly scrolling on their screens. No one is talking. No one is connecting. It's an eerie family meal scenario.

I went to a spin class recently, and when I walked into the

class, there were about eight people already on their bikes, slowly spinning as they waited for class to start. All of them were holding their phones, scrolling along as they stared at the screen. No one looked up. No one greeted me. I quietly got my bike set up for the class and sat bewildered.

What happened to being present?

One of my cool sisters-in-law who is in her early 30s and looks like a CoverGirl model shared an experience of her social media wake-up call. When her oldest child was in kindergarten and was working on homework, my sister-in-law was checking out her social media feed at the table next to the homework set-up. She got entranced in one of those sweet but sad social media stories that make you tear up and want to help the main person in the feed. As she was fixated on this particular story, her son was tugging at her jeans asking for homework help. She was distracted. Once she realized what had happened, she decided to drop social media from her phone. She decided right then and there that she wanted to be present and alive in the moment and wanted to be there for her kids. She hasn't looked back and is one of the most present moms I know—to all six of her crew.

Let's face it. It can be hard today to find balance. We use our phones to communicate, pay bills, order food, watch our favorite shows. Our phones make multitasking seem mindless. Yet, there is that fine line for using them to help our needs and having them counteract our needs.

In 2016 Pope Francis shared this at the Fiftieth World Communication Day: "Emails, text messages, social networks, and chats can also be fully human forms of communication. It is not technology that determines whether or not communication is authentic, but rather the human heart and our capacity to use wisely the means at our disposal."

Discerning how to wisely operate these handy digital helpers is key. Setting healthy boundaries that allow us to remain present with our people will prevent problems. Consider no phones at mealtimes and after a certain time in the evening, all phones get stashed in a drawer to charge and allow the family to experience more face-to-face interactions. Whatever you decide, remember, you are the boss and you set the tech tone in your home.

Summary

STEWARDSHIP OF TIME

As you can see, there are countless opportunities for sharing your time with your family, and they don't have to be difficult! Consider adding any of these to your current daily routines as you continue to answer the Call to Holiness.

- ✝ Pray on the way to school or work
- ✝ Adoration
- ✝ Daily Devotions
- ✝ Divine Mercy Chaplet
- ✝ Rosary
- ✝ Listening to your kids or grandkids
- ✝ Clothes and Conversations (pray for a person whose clothes you're folding)
- ✝ Help after baby is born
- ✝ Help after surgeries
- ✝ Car Conversations (pray while driving)
- ✝ Attend funerals as a family
- ✝ Watch movies with a Christian focus
- ✝ Listen to music with a Christian focus
- ✝ Pray together before bed

"AS EACH ONE
HAS RECEIVED A GIFT,
USE IT TO SERVE ONE
ANOTHER AS GOOD

stewards

OF GOD'S
VARIED GRACE."

— 1 PETER 4:10

STEWARDSHIP OF TALENT
RETURNING OUR GOD-GIVEN GIFTS

The second "T" of the three Stewardship "Ts" is Talent. I have learned firsthand the beauty and blessings that are unleashed from others sharing their God-given talents.

Let me share my lesson.

A few weeks before Eric and I got married, I had my annual medical exam. My doctor told me I would probably not be able to conceive and bear children. My doctor knew my fiancé was part of a large family and knew we wanted a family of our own. He wanted to prepare us for the fact that we might not be able to have children naturally. After the doctor's visit, we were devastated. Young and excited to start our lives building a family, we were not expecting such sad news right before our nuptials.

We headed to daily Mass to pray about this unexpected roadblock. I was 22 and about to graduate college and marry the love of my life. Never once did I consider the inability to bear children. It was shocking.

And, yet, God has a way of shining light into even the darkest corners.

Within six months of our wedding, I was pregnant. Astonished, I couldn't believe it. How could this be? I had just resigned myself to the fact that I would likely not bear my own children and now this abrupt (and joyful) change. It felt a bit like whiplash.

Overjoyed, we celebrated our gift from God. I made sure to eat well, exercise, and be mindful of carrying this precious life inside of me. I had never held a newborn. Honestly, I didn't know very much about babies or children since I only had one sibling and all of my cousins lived thousands of miles away, so I wasn't able to regularly interact with them. To help educate myself on the pregnancy process, I got the popular book, *What to Expect When You're Expecting*, and the geek in me memorized every chapter.

It didn't take long, though, for me to learn that my body didn't adhere to the "regular sections" listed in the book. As a matter of fact, the only section in the book that applied to me was the part titled "Managing a Complicated Pregnancy." Barely into my second trimester, I was baffled by my list of strange symptoms. By week 13, at a wellness visit, the doctor informed me that I was in labor. To those of you who may not know or remember, pregnancy lasts a total of 40 weeks, thus week 13 is way too early to deliver a viable baby. Regardless, here I was two centimeters dilated, 100-percent effaced, and having contractions every five minutes. How could this be? Clearly, I had 27 more weeks to go!

I was terrified.

At that doctor's appointment, I was immediately admitted to the hospital. Rushed into labor and delivery I was given magnesium sulfate through an IV to help all my major muscles relax—including even my eyes—along with multiple narcotics such as morphine to help slow labor down. I couldn't really see or move. I lay in my hospital bed paralyzed. To prevent potential heart issues, I had to have my blood drawn every eight hours to ensure my heart was still safe. For someone who loathes needles and shots, this only brought on additional anxiety counting down the hours to the next pinprick.

Certainly, this wasn't what it was supposed to be like when pregnant.

And, yet, for me, that is what being pregnant meant. Extreme pre-term labor, doctors unable to perform a cerclage due to ongoing contractions that could break my water, and orders to stay laying down (often with a catheter) on strict bed rest or in the hospital until it was safe for baby to arrive. Typically, this meant about six months of bed rest for each pregnancy. I am not speaking about the "bed rest" where you can relax and go shopping. Nope. Attached to an IV and a terbutaline pump, I was "attached" to laying down at home or in the hospital.

In an instant, my entire world changed. I could do nothing for myself and was lying there, watching doctors and nurses and Eric scramble to help me.

I felt completely helpless.

By the grace of God, we made it to week 32 and our oldest daughter, Alanna, was safely born. Weighing over six pounds, she was strong, perfectly healthy, and didn't even need the Neonatal Intensive Care Unit. The nurses said the ongoing trauma in my womb made her resilient. Eric and I knew differently—that sweet, perfect baby was a miracle from God.

After having our eldest, my OB-GYN highly recommended I get my tubes tied or for Eric to get a vasectomy. She explained that having additional children would only exacerbate my "inability to carry a baby to term" condition. We were told we were lucky things ended so well for our firstborn and not to "push our luck." Regardless of their medical suggestion, we remained committed to following Church teaching and chose not to have any procedures to prevent further pregnancies.

True to their words, though, the doctors were correct.

The same thing happened six more times. Two of the pregnancies I miscarried at week 19—almost halfway through the pregnancies, but not far enough for the babies to survive. Those late-term miscarriages were heartbreaking. However, the other four babies were born early but healthy, adding more miracles from God sprinkled into our family.

Through it all, I've spent a total of almost four years of my life strictly hospitalized or bedridden.

During these challenging years, stewardship allowed my family to go on without me.

Literally.

After all, have you ever tried realistically raising a baby or toddler (or worse, tweens and teens) from the bed or without being able to get up? I couldn't even get food for myself, let alone my kiddos.

Completely helpless, I was at the mercy of my family and friends to come to my aid.

WHAT I MISSED

You can imagine all of the events, milestones, and memories I missed while lying in bed. Aside from the day-to-day interactions, I missed those important moments like family and friends' weddings, funerals for those I loved, baptisms of sweet babies, watching my kids perform in sports, school recitals, and award ceremonies. I missed Mass, exercise, and just going outside to get a breath of fresh air.

The list is endless.

One of the toughest events that I missed was when my sister-in-law, Brigid, got married while I was in the hospital. We used to joke that the baby would surely want to arrive the day of the wedding so she wouldn't miss out on all the family fun. Eric was a groomsman in the wedding party and all four of our girls were either junior bridesmaids or flower girls. Everyone was in the wedding party but me. Everyone was at the wedding but me. I have known Brigid since she was 7 years old and she was like a little sister to me. The thought of missing her wedding (which was taking place only a few miles from the hospital I was in at the time) was gut-wrenching.

Before the ceremony, Eric texted me some photos of our girls all dressed up. I remember a particularly special shot of Brigid with our fourth daughter, Anya, who was only 2 at the time. Anya, one of the flower girls, was huddled close to her aunt under the bridal veil. It was a beautiful shot. Then, moments before the Nuptial Mass started, Eric called the hospital room and put Brigid on the phone. The bride could barely utter a "hello" before both of us got all choked up. I told her I loved her and that I was praying for her, and I hung up the phone with tears streaming down my cheeks.

Times like these were especially lonely.

Aside from the bigger misses, there were just the regular days I felt like I didn't know the temperature outside or what season it was. It felt like life was passing me by as I lay in bed. I recall shopping centers being built in my town while I was bedridden. Once I was allowed to get up, I'd be driving around and shocked to see a brand-new strip mall nearby. It was a dark time for me— where I felt disconnected from my friends and family and like a failure as a parent.

Talents I Received

The guilt I felt was immense.

After all, I was literally watching everyone around me "mother" my own children. Although I was beyond grateful to have the help, I was humiliated and felt like a complete burden and, to be honest, defeated.

Msgr. James Costigan is a witty and wise Irish priest friend of our family and was the longtime pastor of our home parish in Augusta. One time, he told me—with that delightful Irish brogue he still retains even after decades of being in America—that my being bedridden was an opportunity for others to come to our aid and serve us. Even though I am more comfortable serving than being served, I soon realized Msgr. Costigan was spot-on. He even practiced what he preached by celebrating Mass in our home while

STEWARDSHIP OF TALENT   88

I was bedridden so that I could attend in person from the couch. It was such a gift to celebrate Mass after being away for so long.

It didn't take long for other help to arrive.

For instance, our meals were prepared and dropped off, groceries were lovingly purchased and provided, I had babysitters lined up for all hours of the day (and some overnights when Eric was traveling), carpooling schedules were created and executed, I had help getting the kids ready for bed, and my clothes were magically washed, dried, folded, and put away. The yard was pruned, our mail was gathered, and our pets were fed.

Homework and project help for the kiddos? Check. School lunches prepared and packed for the children? Check. Birthday parties were planned and executed, and corresponding holiday decorations were put up and taken down. Each week, since I couldn't go to Mass (after all, there was no livestream Mass in 1995, 1996, 1997, 2001, 2006, 2008, and 2010) Eric, who serves as an Extraordinary Minister of Holy Communion, or my father-in-law, who is a deacon, brought me communion.

Not a detail for our family was left undone.

Msgr. Costigan was right.

The millions of opportunities that presented themselves by my inability were all completed by others who stepped in to help us. During those almost four years of being in need, my immediate and extended family filled the front lines. My mom, a true domestic diva, showered us with her household habits to serve us as if we were royalty. Without complaint, before a need arose, she was on it. A true servant, my mother. My mother-in-law, the prayer warrior, with her prayers while pacing around me as I lay in bed in the hospital and at home. Her prayers lifted us. My only sister—a working occupational therapist with five children of her own—still found regular time to assist our family despite her own long list of chores. All of my sisters-in-law and brothers-in-law, despite their schooling, jobs, and families never blinked at lending a regular hand to ensure we were all taken care of. Each time I became pregnant, I felt like it was a "joint effort" as each of them would contribute to filling a need for our growing family.

The sharing of talents did not end with my immediate and extended family members. Through the longevity of it all, friends jumped to my rescue (and my family's rescue) for reinforcement. Neighbors chipped in. School parents and dance parents and soccer parents stepped up to our aid. There were even men and women who helped us that we had never met before. Complete strangers. I distinctly remember one woman bringing us a meal and some cookies who said she heard about our predicament and felt called to help us.

Each of the faces of those who helped us was a light from Christ.

By far, the most remarkable thing to me was that everyone who helped looked so joyful to lend a hand. Instead of making me feel like a burden or being irritated, they had more now on their own plates, they made me feel like it was their pleasure to be a part of my pregnancy. They radiated joy. Joy from sharing their gifts with others.

How would I ever repay the thousands of people who helped?

I could never.

WHAT ARE YOUR TALENTS?

Traveling around and speaking to parishioners about the gift of talent, I often hear people claim they don't have any talents. And, if they do, they don't know what they are.

Really?

There are even companies committed to helping us learn what our talents are.

I am sure for some of us, claiming to have talents may seem like bragging. We don't want to toot our own horns. For others, we see those gifted with certain abilities and may think that since we don't have those specific gifts, maybe we don't have any talents at all. For more of us, when we think of talent, we immediately consider the award-winning actors in movies, prominent singers on the radio or SiriusXM, or well-known athletes playing football, soccer, and baseball on television or in large stadiums. It's easy to identify the gifts of those famous figures. Their gifts are widely recognized and may seem like really huge accomplishments that tower over our smaller abilities.

Don't let that discourage you.

As a matter of fact, I would like to make an important clarification about talents:

I am here to tell you that anything you do in service for another person out of love is a talent!

I have had millions of these "talents" sprinkled on me and my family through the years. I have learned to recognize them as little "presents." Casseroles brought over to feed my family made by a caring neighbor. The mending of my children's clothes by my mom late on a school night when their school uniforms were torn. Having my sister, the occupational therapist, show me how to function with only one arm due to my broken humerus. Having lunch with a close friend who listens to my anxieties and fears and comforts me. These small, typically overlooked types of talents regularly enrich my life.

And probably yours too.

You see, talents don't have to be extraordinary abilities to qualify. Of course, those gigantic talents are also beloved and worthwhile, but talents don't have to be big to count. They simply have to be acts done for others out of love.

The great writer, philosopher, theologian, and famous Catholic convert G.K. Chesterton says this more eloquently than I can with one of his famous quotes: "The most extraordinary thing in the world is an ordinary man and an ordinary woman and their ordinary children."

Living our lives well and sharing our God-given gifts is what it means to live out stewardship. Since God gave us these talents, we aren't meant to hoard them or hide them. We are not meant to sit on them because we may be afraid or embarrassed to put them into action. Nope. We are called to seize the everyday opportunities to let Christ's gifts within us shine.

Saint Mother Teresa says: "Never do the work carelessly because you wish to hide your gifts. Remember, that work is His. You are His co-worker. Therefore, He depends on you for that special work. Do the work with Him, and the work will be done for Him."

While at a silent retreat in the scenic north Georgia mountains in the spring of 2007 with a dear lifelong friend, I found a plaque on the wall above the community dining hall of the rustic retreat house. It caught my attention while sharing a meal with the other attendees (likely since no one could speak). It read:

"Your talent is God's gift to you. What you do with it is your gift back to God."

I am not sure of the author, but the words on that plaque immediately struck me. Was I being a good steward of the gifts God had given me? How many gifts have I given back to God through the years?

I recalled missed opportunities and I felt a tinge of regret. I also remembered times when sharing my gifts lifted others in need and how full I felt doing so. Participating in the ebb and flow of stewardship—the receiving of God's gifts and then giving them away again—allows my hands to always be open and freely receive and then share, again and again.

"FOR WHERE YOUR

treasure is,

THERE ALSO WILL

YOUR HEART BE."

— MATTHEW 6:21

Twelve

STEWARDSHIP OF TREASURE
Giving All of Our Self to God, Including Finances

The Final T of the Three Ts is Treasure, which, not surprisingly, is often the least popular of the three. As I mentioned earlier in the book, this is likely because most people associate the meaning of stewardship with only money or fundraising.

Let's face it, that inaccurate over-association is why this T gets a bad rap.

Hopefully, I can continue to demonstrate the beautiful component of treasure and how it has positively impacted me and my family through the years.

Believe it or not, when not hospitalized or bedridden, Eric and I have been quite involved in parish life. Participating in various ministries has given us great joy and allowed us to share our faith journey in vibrant parishes.

Serving as Extraordinary Ministers of Holy Communion,

speakers for Engaged Couple Weekends in our deanery, leading small faith-sharing groups, serving as lectors, teaching CCD, sponsoring RCIA candidates, being perpetual Adoration adorers, helping with Vacation Bible School, and volunteering at our local Catholic schools, are some of the ways we have connected with parish life over the last 28 years.

As a matter of fact, when we first were married, I honestly believed that since we already "return so much" back to the Church by being involved, we shouldn't have to give back financially. After all, we were giving "practically everything" already.

Of course, this was a lie!

I was fine with tipping my hairdresser or the waitress for their service. However, the idea that I should give back financially to God was easily dismissed since I was already giving all of my time and talents to the Church. Didn't that count? Wasn't that enough?

Eric didn't agree with my thought process. He challenged me from the beginning. When we were young and broke, the idea of giving away even $20 each month terrified me. I clung to our bleak finances like the naïve and untrusting disciple I was at that point. Fearful that if I gave to the weekly offertory, I may not have enough left for groceries or medicine.

Yet, Eric trusted when I did not. He knew that God would see to our every need even when I did not. Moreover, he knew that God calls all of us to give a portion of our finances back in proportion to what we are given. If you are given a small amount, you will return accordingly. And, if you're given a large amount, the same is true.

He would not back down.

Plus, Eric was extremely adamant about not just giving leftover "tips for Jesus." You know, giving a few leftover dollars from your wallet or purse. He wanted us to actually commit to using our offertory envelope each week. Yikes!

Finally, I broke down and gave in. I told him we could put our tithe into our weekly offertory envelope. I had one requirement, though. If during that week we became financially burdened and couldn't purchase a need for our family, then I wouldn't continue giving to the offertory.

Do you know what happened?

We were able to pay for our housing and our food and our medicine. We were even able to have a meal or two out at a restaurant. The world did not end. Life continued the way it always had—even though I gave some of our sparse income away. My fears lessened and we continued using our weekly offertory envelope. Each year, we reassessed where God was calling us to share our financial resources and we then adjusted accordingly. A small tweak here and there. Once I surrendered and gave it a try, I was amazed by the peace and joy it added to my life.

I thank God for Eric, for his shining example of trust. Honestly, I have never missed a penny in almost 30 years. And, God has provided for my every single need. And many, many wants.

INVESTING IN THE CHURCH'S MISSION

There are numerous ways you can take part in sharing your financial resources. My first recommendation is to share them with your parish family. Pray about a good place to start and then commit to giving the same amount each week, if you can. Ensuring your parish has the financial support it needs to feed you spiritually and to extend that support to the surrounding community is a wise choice. If your parish has a school, that would be my second recommendation. After all, those students are the future of the parish and our Catholic faith. Ensuring that they are well-formed is crucial. Sharing resources with the diocese and other Catholic charities is another excellent option. We advise the parishes we work with to encourage parishioners to give five percent to the parish, one percent to the diocese, and four percent to other charities of their choice. It is an easy model to follow. If you can't start with five percent, then start where you can and work your way up when able.

Another creative way to support the Church is to assist missionaries who evangelize locally and globally. A friend of ours started an outreach to Africa where donations are accepted for water wells and livestock to sustain the villages. During liturgical seasons, such as Advent, a family can pick an angel off the Angel Tree or provide a Thanksgiving or Easter Meal to those less fortunate. Choosing these options allows your kids to see you sharing your financial resources firsthand and encourages them to participate, especially if it involves selecting a gift or food items. Also, don't forget about opportunities such as your parish youth group, which may be thrilled to have donations for pizza, snacks, or activities. In addition, consider sponsoring a youth to attend March for Life or a summer missionary camp. I am willing to bet a young person is out there who would like to attend an outreach opportunity but may not have the means to afford it.

The most important thing to remember about our treasure is realizing that it is from God. The brain that God gave us allows us to have a job that provides us with our paycheck. Inviting God into our finances, through prayer and reflecting on how to best budget our resources, is acting as a stellar steward regarding our finances.

Part 2 Summary

TACKLING THE THREE Ts

We are all likely familiar with the common phrase "killing time." Hearing it always makes me cringe since this outlook projects time as something to be wasted, overlooked, or passed to "just get by." As stewards, we recognize that every moment we have on earth is gifted to us from our Heavenly Father. We certainly wouldn't want to "kill" a gift from God, right? Once we realize the blessings of time, our attitude towards how we spend time changes. Instead of wasting the minutes we have been given, we want to fill them with purpose.

When considering the talents that you and your family possess, pray and reflect upon how to best use them to give God glory. If you're unsure of your talents, recall the things that bring you joy. Maybe you enjoy sewing or baking. Maybe you like to work with numbers and help with your family members' taxes or budgeting. Maybe you enjoy working on cars and can fix family members' and friends' cars. If you are still unsure of your talents, consider the things that others compliment in you. Often, these compliments genuinely point to the gifts God has shared with you. The possibilities are endless.

Sharing treasure may seem impossible, especially if your budget is tight. Invite God in. Allow Him to help guide you and how you share your hard-earned dollars. If you order your finances, trusting God to direct their use, He won't disappoint.

THE FOUR PILLARS OF FAMILY STEWARDSHIP

By now, you know stewardship is a gift from God—a way to live as His modern-day disciples in this messy, busy, chaotic world that is integral to family life. It is a way of life that, when truly embraced, brings order, purpose, peace, and deep fulfillment to our families. Be confident as you embrace stewardship at home, knowing you are offering your loved ones a priceless gift.

For stewardship to blossom in our parishes, it must take root within each of the domestic churches that make up the parish family. Parishioners from youngest to oldest must strive to live as Christian stewards every day of the week.

When we speak of stewardship in the parish context, we refer to the four pillars that support a healthy culture of stewardship spirituality. The four pillars are **Hospitality**, **Prayer**, **Formation**, and **Service**.

As we begin this section on the Four Pillars of Stewardship within the family, think about daily life within your "domestic churches." Ask the Holy Spirit to show you the areas of strength in your family life. Which pillar would you say is the strongest in your home? Thank God for this and celebrate it. God does! Also, think about where He may be calling you to even deeper conversion as you strive to live as Christian stewards.

And as we consider the four pillars in the context of our families, let's look to the Holy Family as our inspiration and guide.

"LET ALL GUESTS
WHO ARRIVE
be received
AS CHRIST."

———————

— RULE OF SAINT BENEDICT 53:1

Thirteen

THE FIRST PILLAR: HOSPITALITY

We begin with Hospitality on purpose. We can't expect our family members to pray together, study their faith, and serve others if we have a home where we are disconnected from each other, everyone is off doing their own thing (on their own screens), or the atmosphere is stressful and tense. Of course, we will have moments like this, at least speaking from my own experience. However, we need to be intentional in creating homes where everyone feels cherished, accepted, and important, especially God and His Word.

When building a hospitable environment, it's crucial to remember that hospitality needs to be present whether it is just with your immediate family or for friends and extended family members who visit.

When I first met Eric, I was a college student from a family with one sibling. I grew up with a dinner table of four. Even if my sister and I got to invite a friend over for dinner, we made it to six people—and that was a huge number for us.

After Eric and I had been dating for a short while, he naturally wanted to introduce me to his family, so he invited me to eat dinner with them. I was excited and a bit nervous. I didn't exactly know what to expect, especially as I thought about the differences in the size of our sibling count (remember, he is the oldest of nine).

On the evening of the dinner, Eric picked me up and brought me inside his home. Instantly I saw the distinctions. Where my home was quiet and orderly, Eric's home was vibrant and chaotic. As we entered the dining room, I took one look at the dining room table and was shocked. Instead of my usual four place settings, there were 12. Twelve! I was astonished. Eric's parents entered and Eric made the introductions. They graciously invited me to sit down and break bread with the entire family and I must admit it felt surreal. As I watched the food being dished out and passed around and as I watched the siblings quietly quibble over an extra roll, all I could think was that Eric's mom did this three times a day, every day, year-round! In one year, that equates to feeding 11 people almost 1,100 meals. I was amazed. Clearly, she was already a saint undertaking the nutritional needs of nine children and a husband daily with no cook or maid to help. I was in awe. Then, to add to her workload was an extra place for me. I felt bad. She already had so much to do, and my presence was adding more preparations and more work.

Not once did she (or any of the family) make me feel like a burden. The natural rhythm they established from their regular family meal routine was pleasant and even though it was a bit overwhelming to witness, I enjoyed every bit. I left feeling full of food, but also full of something else—I couldn't put my finger on it, but looking back on it, I now recognize it as hospitality.

Two days later, I received a thank you card in the mail. It was from Eric's mom, and it read:

Dear Lisa,

Thank you for joining us for dinner last night. It was lovely to meet you. You are welcome back anytime, no matter how many people are here.

Love,
Pat McArdle

I still have the card in a special box. Despite nourishing nine children and a ton of dishes, she found time to ensure I felt welcomed in her home. To this day, I always feel welcome.

"IT IS EASY TO LOVE THE PEOPLE FAR AWAY. IT IS NOT ALWAYS EASY TO LOVE THOSE CLOSE TO US. IT IS EASIER TO GIVE A CUP OF RICE TO RELIEVE HUNGER THAN TO RELIEVE THE LONELINESS AND PAIN OF SOMEONE UNLOVED IN OUR OWN HOME. BRING LOVE INTO YOUR HOME, FOR THIS IS WHERE OUR LOVE FOR *each other* MUST START."

— SAINT MOTHER TERESA

HOSPITALITY (HALTS) AT HOME

Why is it so much easier to be polite and patient with colleagues at work or even strangers in the grocery store than it is to be so with our own family members? At least speaking for myself, that is. It is easy to take those we live with for granted because, well, we live with them. We see each other with bedhead and morning breath. When we get home at the end of a long day, we want to kick off our shoes and let our guard down. And that's okay.

We are our most vulnerable selves when we are at home. But that is all the more reason to practice hospitality first and foremost within our family life. We want our homes to be an oasis of peace and comfort from the crazy world outside, a place where we can be loved simply for who we are and not what we accomplish or produce. That is how God loves us.

We also want our homes to be the place where we can get recharged and filled up to go out and bring love to everyone we encounter outside our home. That is why hospitality must be a pillar of our family life, starting with the way that we treat each other within the home.

What do you think of when you hear the word "hospitality?" These phrases may come to mind:

Saying "Please and Thank you."

Saying "I'm sorry."

Saying "I forgive you."

Saying "You're welcome here! Come in!"

However, far deeper than good manners or a superficial exchange of pleasantries, **the virtue of hospitality is the outward expression of seeing people as God sees them, of readiness to welcome others into our lives whenever and however God asks us to do so.**

In other words, Christian hospitality is an attitude or posture we take with us wherever we go, whether at home with our loved ones, welcoming visitors into our homes or parish, or when we are out and about at work, school, or in the community. If we are willing to practice true, Christian hospitality in our daily lives, our families, workplaces, and our parish can be transformed.

"BEHOLD, I AM THE
HANDMAID OF THE LORD.
MAY IT BE DONE TO ME

according

TO YOUR WORD."

———

— LUKE 1:38

HOLY FAMILY
HOSPITALITY

Let's reflect on the very best family model, the Holy Family, and how they lived hospitality.

BLESSED MOTHER

In Luke 1:28-45, we read about the Annunciation. The Angel Gabriel suddenly shows up in Mary's room to offer her an extraordinary invitation. And she quickly says, "Yes!" Specifically, she says: "Behold, I am the handmaid of the Lord. May it be done to me according to your word." (Luke 1:38).

Imagine being a young woman and having an angel approach you. I don't know about you, but I would be extremely shocked and frightened in that situation. Then, hearing something unimaginable, Mary doesn't even have to ask to think it over. Although she does ask, "How can this be?" she doesn't pause to consider how radically altered her life will be by partaking in such a request. She doesn't weigh the risk involved. Also, she doesn't present excuses of how someone older and more mature would be a better candidate.

Mary's attitude, her whole being, is one of hospitality and openness to God's plan for her life and for the others He wants her to welcome into her life. She immediately welcomes Jesus when the Father asks her to. She immediately welcomes all of us when Jesus asks this of her on the Cross through His giving of her to the care of John and John to her.

Wow. What a witness of hospitality!

When I was pregnant the seventh time, I was devastated. This wasn't my first rodeo, and I knew what this pregnancy promised for my family and me. Although I was open to life and thrilled by the gift of a new addition to the family, deep down, I was exhausted at the thought of enduring another bed rest and hospitalization. Several of my close friends were eager to get pregnant and I couldn't help thinking "Why not them, Lord?" As the weeks went on, my exhaustion and frustration grew, and before long, I became angry. Really angry. I kept asking, "Why?" My pity party continued until my wise sister dropped by our house to encourage me. She gently shared the Annunciation passage with me, prayed with me, and then asked me to think of Mary's fiat as inspiration.

Not long after her visit, I realized I was operating in selfish mode and not living as a good steward. I was not open to God's plan. I was not grateful and accepting. Nope. I was closed to His plan and not willing to hospitably welcome His gift—in this case, a sweet baby. Instead, my fists were angrily clenched, and I cried and yelled with resistance.

In time, my sister's plan of sharing about Mary's fiat helped me to recenter. I wanted to emulate Mary's example, even if it was difficult. The 40 days straight I stayed in the hospital for that particular pregnancy were more peaceful than any of the previous durations. Being open to God's plan (instead of fighting it) brought me a sense of tranquility I had never experienced before.

What a contrast my response was to the pregnancy compared to Mary's! Just when I thought I was getting the hang of stewardship, I slipped the second I was inconvenienced. Thank goodness for such a shining light to follow with Mary.

SAINT JOSEPH

Now let's consider Saint Joseph, his hospitality, and his openness to God's plan for his life throughout the context of Matthew 1:18-25.

Every episode of Joseph's life is a crisis. He discovers that the woman to whom he was betrothed is pregnant. He resolves to divorce her quietly, but then the angel of the Lord appears in a dream and explains the anomalous pregnancy. Now that he understands what is happening in the context of God's providence, Joseph does as the angel commands him and "takes Mary into his home."

Joseph is always listening and attentive to the leading of the Holy Spirit for his family. It is Joseph who finds the stable (or more likely the cave) where the baby Jesus would be born. No doubt it is Joseph who cleans it up and prepares it for Mary and Jesus since we know that Mary is great with child. Saint Joseph protects them, guards them, tends to their safety, their comfort, and their well-being at the expense of his own plans and preferences.

Next, discovering that the child is in mortal danger, Joseph takes mother and baby on a perilous journey to an unknown country.

Anyone who has ever been forced to move to a new city knows the anxiety that Joseph must have felt. But Joseph goes because God had commanded him.

Later, in Luke 2:45-50, we learn of Joseph desperately seeking his lost 12-year-old son. Quietly taking the child home, Joseph once more puts aside his human feelings and trusts in the purposes of God.

The little we know about Joseph is that he experiences heartbreak, fear unto death, and a parent's deepest anxiety. But each time, he reads what happened to him as a Theo-drama, not an ego-drama. This shift in attitude is what makes Joseph the patron of the Universal Church.

This is masculine hospitality. We do not hear any words from Saint Joseph at all. But his actions show that he is open to the guidance of the Holy Spirit and offers himself to his family. And his family thrives and does all it is called to do, becoming all it is meant to become for the world in large part because of Saint Joseph's strong guidance and ongoing protection for them.

After the birth of our Lord, the Holy Parents could have closed off that stable to just enjoy their Son, to keep Him safe and away from outside eyes, at least for a little while. But they do just the opposite. They share their humble, makeshift home and their newborn Son immediately with the world. They welcome each guest with the same dignity and gratitude and warmth—both humble shepherd and great wise kings. Mary sees the beauty in each of the visitors as she ponders their presence in her heart. Mary sees the goodness in them. She sees it in us, too.

This is how God is calling our families to live hospitality. Like Mary and Joseph's examples, we are to be the servants of the Lord.

"WELCOME ONE ANOTHER,
THEN, AS CHRIST
welcomed you,
FOR THE GLORY OF GOD."

———

— ROMANS 15:7

HOSPITALITY
AT HOME

H ere are some practical ideas to get us reflecting on highlighting hospitality within the walls of our homes.

HOSPITALITY HOME ATTITUDE

Make it a goal to sit down to eat together as a family as much as possible. Take this time to find out about each other's day—the high and low of the day, each other's biggest challenges, something funny that happened, or even something surprising. Then, listen to each other's responses.

FOCUS (ON PEOPLE, NOT SCREENS)

When your spouse or kids are talking to you, look them in the eye. Put down the phone, iPad, or computer, and be sure to give them your full attention.

SPECIAL MEALS

Make Sunday dinner or lunches special—or whatever day works best for the majority of the family. Make a favorite dessert. Put on some music in the background. Encourage everyone to attend to cherish time together. Make the same effort to celebrate family birthdays, baptismal days, sacraments, etc. The dinner table is a great place to connect and recharge with our loved ones. And, if you're not a big fan of cooking in the kitchen, eating take-out at the table counts too!

BUILDING UP INSIDE THE WALLS

Families are meant to support one another. So, no "one-upping" allowed. We don't put other family members down; instead, we always build our family members up. Joking is fine, of course, and often a great way to laugh together.

MIND YOUR MANNERS

Sure, hospitality is deeper than good manners, but it does include good manners—even to those we live most closely with. Saying things like "Please," "Thank you," "May I," "I'm sorry," and "Please forgive me" goes such a long way in fostering a loving atmosphere at home.

HOSPITALITY TOWARDS GUESTS IN OUR HOME

Make guests of all ages feel welcome and important. Ask them about themselves. Put guests at ease and make them feel like part of the family. As Saint Benedict says, "Receive them as Christ."

HOSPITALITY WHEN "OUT AND ABOUT"

Remember to leave home with the same attitude as you have at home—warmth towards others, making people feel at ease and important in your presence, going out of your way to smile, to offer help, look people in the eye, and even let someone get ahead of you in the checkout line. Challenge yourself to make one positive connection with a stranger every time you leave the house.

Let's resolve to practice Christian hospitality towards everyone we encounter, starting right at home. Let us pray that God will open our minds and soften our hearts to those around us so that we are ready to set aside our own plans for their sake, find the goodness within them, and call it forth as Jesus does for each one of us. In this "give and take" of hospitality in family life, we have the opportunity to grow and become more and more like Jesus.

"PRAYER IS NOTHING ELSE
THAN BEING ON TERMS OF

friendship

WITH GOD."

———

— SAINT TERESA OF AVILA

14

Fourteen

THE SECOND PILLAR: PRAYER

The Second Pillar of Stewardship is Prayer. Prayer teaches us how to listen and speak to God, and to live in intimate relationship with Him.

Likely all of us are familiar with prayer. However, some of us may be more comfortable than others with praying, as I've discovered through over 20 years of conducting parish surveys. For instance, the surveys have revealed that some of us are intimidated about praying. After all, it is easy to pray along in church, where we recite prayers with our parish family during Mass. However, we may not exactly know what to do when we are at home alone. Is there a roadmap? Is there a wrong way to pray? Also, how do we properly pray with our families? It may be easy for us to pray by ourselves; however, praying may become challenging when we try to do so with our spouses, children, or grandchildren.

Do not fear! Prayer is not meant to confound us or scare us. It is simply a way to converse with God. A few definitions from the saints can help demonstrate the simplicity to which I am referring:

Saint John Vianney says, "Prayer is nothing less than union with God."

Saint Therese says, "I pray like children who do not know how to read. I say very simply to God what I wish to say without composing beautiful sentences and He always understands me."

Prayer doesn't need to be complicated. And, especially in family life, generally, the simpler, the better. If it is simple, you will be more likely to make it a natural part of life.

Isn't that great news?

And, even beginning simply, prayer is a powerful practice that can help us all with our ultimate goal as stewards—to spend eternity with God in heaven.

Saint Ephraim says, "Virtues are formed by prayer. Prayer preserves temperance. Prayer suppresses anger. Prayer prevents emotions of pride and envy. Prayer draws into the soul of the Holy Spirit and raises man to Heaven."

"LOVE BEGINS IN
OUR HOME BY
praying
TOGETHER."

— SAINT MOTHER TERESA

12

PRAYING WITH
THE HOLY FAMILY

Again, let's look to the Holy Family for inspiration. Each time we hear about the "growing up" years of Jesus, it is in the context of the Holy Family living out their faith as a family.

Joseph and Mary knew their Son was God but still carefully observed the faith practices of their day. For instance, they followed the custom of the Presentation in the Temple. Even the God-man was not exempt from the traditions of the faith. His parents took His faith formation seriously and note that Jesus was obedient to His parents. Stewardship applies to kids, too!

It's amazing to think that the first 30 of our Lord's 33 years of life on earth were spent in the context of ordinary family life. Even Jesus' first miracle happened at the Wedding of Cana, where His mother encouraged Him to act. Clearly, marriage and family life are important to the Holy Family and our Heavenly Father.

"AND MARY KEPT ALL
THESE THINGS,

reflecting

ON THEM IN
HER HEART."

—————

— LUKE 2:19

MOTHER MARY

We can learn much from considering Mother Mary's prayer life.

In Luke 2:51, we read that Mary "kept all these things in her heart." Mary's prayer life happened in the midst of family life. She took all the events of the day and brought them to the Heavenly Father to talk them over and reflect on them with Him. That's prayer. We can all do that. The Holy Spirit is very active in our own lives; we just need to take the time to ponder like Mary. Give yourself permission to ponder and treasure things in your heart.

"I PRAY LIKE CHILDREN
WHO DO NOT KNOW HOW
TO READ. I SAY VERY
SIMPLY TO GOD WHAT I
WISH TO SAY WITHOUT
COMPOSING BEAUTIFUL
SENTENCES AND

He always

UNDERSTANDS ME."

— SAINT THERESE OF LISIEUX

12

GETTING STARTED

God created within each one of us the need to pray. After all, God doesn't need our prayers, but we possess a longing to pray, to adore Him, and to thank Him.

To get started praying, consider using the ACTS method. This method helps you easily remember four types of prayer to incorporate into your daily prayer time.

<u>A</u>doration: Praising God for who He is

<u>C</u>ontrition: Asking God for forgiveness for faults

<u>T</u>hanksgiving: Thanking God for blessings (and challenges)

<u>S</u>upplication: Asking God for help (for self and on behalf of others, technically intercession)

In addition to recalling and incorporating these four types of prayers, here are some other helpful strategies to aid us while praying at home.

TIMES FOR PRAYER

Think about strategic times to incorporate these different types of prayer. Consider praying in the car if you drive kids to school and activities, or a simple blessing on the forehead before they head out the door. Mealtime is a great time for prayer. Also, don't forget evening prayers before lights out.

ESTABLISHING A ROUTINE

It is helpful to have a method so everyone knows what to expect. However, it is also good to let it evolve, and it is definitely important to be flexible. Establish a routine for mornings, evening prayers, and "short prayers" in a pinch. There is no right or wrong way. Remember, you do want it to be sincere and not just perfunctory to get it over with.

MORNING HOURS

Start by making an offering of the day followed by a spontaneous prayer of praise. Then, share something you are thankful for and ask forgiveness if we are short-tempered getting out the door.

EVENING HOURS

Consider reading the Gospel Reflection for the day or saying a decade of the Rosary. Another great option is the Guardian Angel prayer and ending with an Act of Contrition. For younger ones, simply saying "I thank you, Jesus, for... (thanksgiving)" and "I love you, Jesus, because... (praise) are great options.

OTHER PRAYERFUL IDEAS

Consider keeping a family prayer journal. It becomes a fun family record through the years. You can include answered prayers as well as requests. Reviewing it will showcase how many prayers have been answered, especially if they are in unexpected ways.

FAMILY DEVOTIONS

Does your family have a devotion? Have you ever considered one such as to the Sacred Heart, or Divine Mercy, etc? These devotions help to give a focus to one's prayers and strengthen family identity.

OLDER CHILDREN

For those of us with adult children, prayer time is going to look a bit different than for those of us with littles still under our roof. Often, in this new stage of parenthood with adult children, the most important act of parental stewardship we can give them is our prayers for them.

SUMMARY: JUST DO IT!

Family prayer does not need to be long or complicated. But do establish it as a habit—a pillar of your family life—no matter the resistance you may receive or how often you get off track. Remember our prayer time will form us to be saints. It is so worth it and every effort to draw near to the Lord will please our gracious God who wants so much to be close to you in the ups and downs of family life.

HOW WILL I KNOW IF GOD HEARS MY PRAYER?

Saint Monica prayed almost her entire life for the conversion of her son, Saint Augustine. Her persistence, her faith, and her trust in God helped her steadfastly pray for her wayward son. Eventually, her prayers were answered, and her son not only converted to the Catholic faith, but also became a Doctor of the Church.

Like Mary and Joseph and Monica, we are called to pray for our families and those entrusted to our care. How will we know that God hears us? How will we know that we will impact those we pray for?

The short answer is, we won't.

Not all prayers will be answered in the way we see fit. However, all prayers will be answered in the way God sees best. Trusting God is the key!

Saint Mother Teresa, who exhibited unwavering faith through her trials and tribulations, shares some wisdom regarding how our daily lives and prayers influence and impact those we love—even if we don't receive a concrete answer.

She says:

> "You will teach them to fly, but they will not fly your flight.
> You will teach them to dream, but they will not dream your dream.
> You will teach them to live, but they will not live your life.
> Nevertheless, in every flight, in every life, in every dream,
> the print of the way you taught them will remain."

God has gifted us with our families—our children, our nieces and nephews, our godchildren, our grandchildren, and our great-grandchildren—and we are called to pray for them, to guide them on their faith walk, and to help them blossom in holiness.

"LEARN THE HEART
OF GOD FROM THE

Word

OF GOD."

— SAINT POPE GREGORY THE GREAT

Fifteen

THE THIRD PILLAR:
FORMATION

The Third Pillar of Stewardship is Formation. Formation teaches us to know and love our God *and* our faith. According to the United States Conference of Catholic Bishops' *National Directory for Catechesis* (2005, #20), there are six tasks of faith formation that constitute a unified whole by which faith formation seeks to achieve its objective. This primary objective is the formation of disciples of Jesus Christ.

The six tasks of formation promote knowledge of the faith, promote knowledge of the meaning of the liturgy and the sacraments, promote moral formation in Jesus Christ, teach us how to pray, prepare one to live in community, and participate actively in the life of the Church, and promote a missionary spirit that prepares one to be present as Christians in society.

Take a moment to consider how fully you are currently formed.

When is the last time you read a book about the Catholic faith? When is the last time you participated in a Bible study? When is the last time you read and reflected on the readings before Mass? Or looked up something in the *Catechism*?

Frequently, through our parish survey responses, I find that the last faith formation parishioners receive dates back to when they completed their Confirmation preparation or attended their last religious formation class as a middle or high school student. This means decades may have gone by since parishioners and family members have experienced formation.

If that is the last time you have formed yourself or that members of your families have formed themselves, don't panic. You are not alone.

This realization is an opportunity for growth. It's a chance to dip your toe back in the water of faith formation and even to learn alongside the members of your family, including the youngest members who are also learning. Don't ever feel embarrassed that you don't know an answer to the faith questions asked to you by your children or grandchildren. Instead, learn together!

Remember, the more fully you are formed, the better you will understand God's calling for your family. Furthermore, the more you are formed in the faith, the easier it will be to answer the call of discipleship.

"DO WHATEVER HE

tells you."

— JOHN 2:5

⊥3⊥

FORMING OURSELVES
TO FIND GOD'S PLAN

Being properly formed in our faith and listening to God's call allows us to understand if we are on the right path or if we need to redirect. Being prayerful and well-formed are key to our following His plan for our lives instead of our own wishes and desires. Remember, as stewards, we strive to listen to God and use the gifts He has given us to serve those he places in our paths.

Thankfully, it is easier now more than ever to form ourselves and our families.

There is no need to search for faith-formation opportunities. These options can be sent directly to our smartphones and tablets. Bishop Barron's *Word on Fire* ministry sends free daily readings along with a brief Gospel reflection straight to our inboxes. Matthew Kelly's *Dynamic Catholic* offers Lenten and Advent opportunities with free, reflective videos that also arrive via email. *Blessed is She* even provides an endearing female faith formation perspective—perfect for women young and old. Plus, if you want to form yourself specifically in Scripture, you can also opt for the free podcast, *The Bible in a Year*, featuring the entertaining Fr. Mike Schmitz, from Ascension Presents. Honestly, the possibilities are endless.

Formation is the fuel that keeps your family moving forward as stewards and in becoming all that Christ is calling you to be. Have confidence as you incorporate this ongoing learning into your daily routines.

"OUR CONCERN MUST BE
TO KNOW GOD'S WILL. WE
MUST ENTER THAT PATH:
IF GOD WANTS. WHEN

God wants.

HOW GOD WANTS."

— SAINT GIANNA BERETTA MOLLA

FOLLOWING GOD'S WILL — EVEN WHEN IT DOESN'T MAKE SENSE

Saint Gianna Beretta Molla genuinely understands this principle. She states: **"Our concern must be to know God's Will. We must enter that path: If God wants. When God wants. How God wants."**

What would our lives look like if we followed this mantra?

When I was a senior in high school, my father, a mechanical engineer, lost his job at our local power plant because the plant was mothballed. Instead of moving to another plant out of state for my senior year, my parents opted to find odd jobs for my dad to do locally. This meant money was tight. So, for college, I had to look for a college scholarship. I was fortunate to earn a journalism scholarship at the University of Georgia (UGA) in Athens, and the scholarship meant I could attend college without added financial burden for my parents.

Midway through my time in Athens, I received a call from my parents. They told me my dad was able to find a great contract job in New York. Instead of leaving my sister alone in our hometown of Augusta while she attended the Medical College of Georgia (also in Augusta), they wanted me to return to our hometown and attend the local university so we could be together. Since we had no other family nearby, my parents said it would bring them peace knowing we were together. They even offered to put us both up in an apartment.

I was so confused. I had earned this scholarship at an incredible university. Why would I leave? I took it to prayer. Sneaking into the UGA Newman Center, I prayed about it, asking God to help with my decision. I asked God, "What should I do?" Do you know what I heard in reply? "Go home, Lisa." Clearly, I wasn't hearing properly. Wasn't the scholarship to UGA an answer to prayer in the first place? Why on earth would God want me to return before receiving my degree? So, the next day, I popped in and prayed, asking the same question to find out what to do. Again, I heard, "Go home, Lisa."

And so, at the end of that school term, I packed up and went back to Augusta to enroll in Augusta State University and move into an apartment with my sister. My parents moved to New York feeling peaceful my sister and I were together and had each other nearby. Do you know what happened two weeks later?

I met Eric.

Two months after, we introduced my sister to her now-husband of 25 years.

I did whatever God told me, and I ended up in the right place at the right time doing what God had willed for me. Of course, it didn't make sense at the time, but it sure does now.

"MAY WE ALLOW OURSELVES
TO BE LED BY THE HOLY
SPIRIT TO AN EVEN
greater love
OF THE WORD OF GOD."

— POPE BENEDICT XVI

FAMILY FORMATION IDEAS

Just as with prayer, it is okay and even preferable to keep formation times simple. Use holy days, sacrament days, and even holidays to work formation into the natural rhythms of family life. Take baby steps.

Here are some practical ideas to get started with ongoing faith formation:

CELEBRATE FEAST DAYS AND SAINT DAYS

Have you ever considered celebrating the Feast of the Guardian Angels, feast days devoted to the Blessed Mother, the Feast of the Sacred Heart, Pentecost, or the Feast of the Holy Family? Keep it simple with a meal or just dessert, adding a tablecloth on the table with a few flowers, and reading together a little about the feast. That's it! A friend of mine keeps a box of brownie mix on hand or has her kids make the dessert. It's super simple but establishes Catholic culture in-home and forms our kids and grandkids in the faith.

SECULAR CELEBRATIONS

Thanksgiving and birthdays can also be used as opportunities for formation. During November, you can share what you are thankful for—something different every day. Also, Thanksgiving is a great time to attend Mass to express gratitude for all the blessings God has bestowed on us. One of our daughters' birthdays falls on the Feast of the Immaculate Conception and we regularly share about the significance. We even gave her a Marian name to honor the Blessed Mother.

LENT

Lent is a great time for incorporating family faith formation. Consider placing a crown of thorns on the kitchen counter or table, attend Stations of the Cross as a family, and ponder a family Lenten sacrifice in *addition* to individual sacrifice. Don't forget to celebrate the Triduum—Holy Thursday, Good Friday, and Holy Saturday—as a family and talk about the significance of each liturgy. Read the Sunday Gospel each week before going to Mass.

EASTER

The biggest feast of the Catholic Church is the Easter season, which is 50 days. Use this time to celebrate the joys of the Resurrection with your family—with food, faith-filled activities, and family time together. Celebrate the end of the Easter season by wishing the Church "Happy Birthday" on Pentecost!

ADVENT

Advent is another great liturgical option to form our families. Utilize an Advent wreath at the kitchen table. Participate in "Straws in the Manger," where you place a straw in the manger each time a good deed is completed. Have a "Jesus" stocking, asking family members to answer, "How did I emulate Jesus today?" Also, consider learning about the "O" antiphons and what they teach us.

CHRISTMAS

Don't forget that Christmas is more than just one day! Instead, celebrate *all* the days of Christmas. Have a family celebration on the Feast of the Holy Family, do a blessing of the Christmas gifts before opening them, or have a sibling exchange of gifts. Don't forget to bless doors with chalk on Epiphany.

OTHER OPTIONS

✝ Keep the *Catechism* handy to look up when you don't know an answer and learn together!

✝ Ask kids and grandkids what they are learning in religion or CCD.

✝ Go to Confession as a family.

✝ Watch faith-based movies together as a family.

✝ Live out Sundays as a true day of rest together.

"TO MAINTAIN A JOYFUL
FAMILY REQUIRES MUCH
FROM BOTH THE PARENTS
AND THE CHILDREN.
EACH MEMBER OF THE
FAMILY HAS TO BECOME
IN A SPECIAL WAY

the servant

OF THE OTHERS."

— SAINT POPE GREGORY THE GREAT

4

Sixteen

THE FOURTH PILLAR: SERVICE

The Fourth Pillar of Stewardship—Service—is an opportunity for the family to put into concrete action the three pillars we have already reflected on—hospitality, prayer, and formation. When a family serves out of convictions that have been forged through an attitude of hospitality, an active prayer life, and strong formation in the faith, that service will have a great impact on both the ones doing the serving *and* the ones being served. Why? The answer is simple.

It will be Christ-like service, which is the mission of the Church.

This type of genuine service isn't done to get attention or applause and it is not done to get something in return. Instead, this type of service is simply done in imitation of our brother and Savior, Jesus Christ, out of a spirit of grateful obedience for all the blessings

God has given us. This means that even very small acts of service can make a huge difference.

Recently, I had such an unexpected experience.

My 99-year-old grandmother grew up in Thompson, North Dakota, and has lived in nearby Grand Forks, North Dakota, independently for the last three decades. Through the years, Eric and I, along with my parents and sister, have asked her time and time again to move down to the south so she could be close to our family.

My grandma always gave us the same answer: No. She thanked us for offering but said North Dakota was her home, and she couldn't consider leaving. Although we understood her connection, we were sad that we couldn't regularly see someone that lived 1,588 miles away.

In late 2019, however, my grandmother had a minor fall that made her reconsider. Not having any family nearby to help when a need arose made her realize it was time to accept our offer and move to the Peach State. My dad eagerly flew to North Dakota, packed her up, and flew her back to her new home. Having my grandma nearby has opened up a whole new world of possibilities.

As an Extraordinary Minister of Holy Communion, I have been privileged to bring the Body of Christ to those who couldn't attend Mass. However, I never had the honor of bringing it to my grandmother. All that changed once she arrived. Now, I regularly bring Jesus to her, and then we enjoy lunch together. It gives me time to reconnect and savor the memories she shares about her childhood and my dad's early years spent on their family farm. This tiny act of service has given me far more blessings than I anticipated. Even though it is a small act of service for her, it is really a huge gift to me!

"FOR EVEN AS THE
SON OF MAN DID NOT
COME TO BE SERVED,
BUT TO SERVE, AND TO
GIVE HIS LIFE AS

a ransom

FOR MANY."

— MARK 10:45

THE HOLY FAMILY SERVES

L et's turn to the Holy Family one more time for examples of service:

JOSEPH'S SERVICE

Saint Joseph's whole life is spent in service to his family. Joseph keeps Jesus and Mary safe, protected, and sheltered. He teaches Jesus his trade of carpentry. These small acts of service are critical to the mission of the Holy Family. Contemplating these endeavors elevates the dignity of family life.

THE VISITATION

After the Angel Gabriel visits Mary and she says "yes" to his incredible offer, Mary makes haste to visit her cousin Elizabeth, who Mary learns is also expecting. Elizabeth is Mary's older cousin who was believed to be too old to conceive. Despite a long and likely grueling journey, Mary chooses to be with her cousin. She wishes to share her love and presence with her relative and to serve her in her time of need. Elizabeth's response to Mary's arrival is: "And how does this happen to me, that the mother of my Lord should come to me?" (Luke 1:43). Even Elizabeth's baby in the womb (John the Baptist) recognizes Mary's act of service in coming to visit Elizabeth and he leaps in her womb—a unique expression of hospitality.

WEDDING FEAST AT CANA

Another example of the Blessed Mother in service occurs at Jesus' first miracle at the Wedding Feast at Cana. Mary notices the wine has run out. She wants to preserve the dignity of the hosts and wants to keep the celebration going. Mary accomplishes this humbly, graciously, and unobtrusively. A harmony of service and hospitality are in play as Mary acts. She pays attention to the details of life that make things comfortable and welcoming for those around her. She does a little thing that makes a huge difference. Not in an intrusive way, but in a loving, gracious understated way. Mary says to the wine steward, "Do whatever He tells you." This is my favorite part of the story because she gets her child to do the actual serving. Also, notice it is a steward who does the serving and helps with the miracle!

In the U.S. Conference of Catholic Bishops' Pastoral Letter on stewardship, *Stewardship: A Disciple's Response*, the bishops remind us that Mary is the epitome of stewardship: "After Jesus, it is the Blessed Virgin Mary who by her example most perfectly teaches the meaning of discipleship and stewardship in their fullest sense... she was called and gifted by God; she responded generously, creatively, and prudently; she understood her divinely assigned role in terms of service and fidelity."

CHARITY AND THE HOME TEAM

The first "mission field" of service, of course, is our own homes. Thus, the pillar of service in the family begins right within our own homes. We must have a servant's heart like Jesus towards those we live most closely with. This means that mom and dad are not only the family servants. Mom, dad, brothers, and sisters are a team that works together for the common good of the whole family.

HELPING THE HOMELESS

In 2011 our family helped at a local homeless shelter that served hot meals. Once a month, we would head down to the shelter, prep the food in the kitchen, prepare it for serving, serve the food to the people in line and clean up afterward. It was a full day, but a rewarding day to share with our girls. In order to participate at the shelter, you had to be 10 years old, so when our middle daughter, Ashlin, turned 10, she couldn't wait to join her two big sisters in action.

This particular winter Sunday, the temperature in our southern town was extra chilly and we had to break out our wool coats, which is rare for us, even in the winter. This made Ashlin extremely happy since she got to wear her favorite red wool coat. It buttoned up the front and looked a bit like the "Madeline" coat featured in the children's book. Skipping to the shelter, we entered, hung up our jackets, and started on our kitchen duties. Ashlin beamed as she got to participate in small kitchen tasks, dishing out the food and helping to gather the used dishes for washing. At the end of the day, she looked a bit tired but fulfilled.

As we headed to grab our coats on the way out of the building Ashlin noticed that her coat was no longer on the hook next to the rest of our coats. Bewildered, we all looked around thinking maybe it was misplaced.

Without missing a beat, Ashlin came up to me, looked me straight in the eyes, and exclaimed, "Someone must have needed the coat today more than me, Mom." She smiled and looked satisfied that her coat would also serve some other girl in need. Ashlin understood why we were there, and she understood what those homeless people needed. I didn't need to teach Ashlin anything. That day, *she* taught *me!*

"BE WHO GOD CREATED
YOU TO BE AND YOU WILL
SET THE WORLD ON

fire."

— SAINT CATHERINE OF SIENA

FAMILY SERVICE IDEAS

Remember that service is not just for the grown-ups. Everyone should aim to have a parish ministry (or more) to which they are committed. Help your kids find one that works for them. Be open to ministries you may not have considered before—the Holy Spirit is always at work in our lives, guiding us to more growth. Also, it's great if the family can participate together.

SERVICE TO THE WIDER COMMUNITY (LOCAL AND GLOBAL)

Service can be something the whole family does together and can be through the parish if there are such ministries. We are globally connected now, thanks to modern technology. Help your kids to see how blessed they are to live in this country, and in their particular neighborhood, and then give to others in gratitude for their blessings.

OTHER POSSIBILITIES TO CONSIDER:

✝ Commit to serving at a parish event or in a ministry as a family—you will be using your talents and bonding as a family at the same time!

✝ Make service to the parish and community a family tradition so that all members of the household (kids included!) are expected to commit to some form of ministry participation.

✝ Parents and children alike can commit to one extra act of service to a family member every day (doing a siblings' chore, reading to a young one, coloring a picture for a grandparent).

✝ If you are homebound, consider ways you can serve right from home—helping with phone calls or emails for a ministry or offering skills like sewing or baking for parish events.

✝ Make your home itself a place of ministry. Invite a lonely neighbor or a new parishioner over for coffee or dinner each month.

Part 3 Summary

IT'S TIME TO GET PERSONAL

Now comes the important part: the part where you take these themes—these jumping-off spots to the Holy Spirit—and see where He wants to take you with them regarding hospitality, prayer, formation, and service.

Ask the Holy Family to become your mentors and guides. They will surround you with their love and peace and help you to become the good stewards God has meant to be. And you and your families will set the world on fire!

"LET EACH FATHER MAKE HIS HOME A CHURCH. ARE YOU NOT RESPONSIBLE FOR THE SALVATION OF YOUR CHILDREN? ARE YOU NOT LIKELY TO GIVE AN ACCOUNT FOR THEIR UPBRINGING? JUST AS CLERGY WILL GIVE AN ACCOUNT FOR THEIR FLOCKS, SO FATHERS [AND MOTHERS] OF FAMILIES WILL HAVE TO ANSWER BEFORE GOD FOR *all the people* IN THEIR HOME."

— SAINT JOHN CHRYSOSTOM

WHAT ARE YOU WAITING FOR?

Have you ever read Mathew Kelly's book, *The Biggest Lie in The History of Christianity*?

If not, do you know what the biggest lie ever told is?

As Catholics, we believe we cannot attain holiness. That we cannot be disciples. We aren't "good" enough or "capable" enough. Satan is telling us that lie. Satan is preventing us from growing in God's confidence and call to "Follow Me" and gear our families to be intentional disciples.

Do you believe that lie too?

If so, it's time you rolled up your sleeves and changed course. It's time to rewrite the book your children and grandchildren are reading about your family. Stewardship allows you to craft the story you want them to follow. The way to live your life in a grateful and joyful manner. A way that allows you to utilize your God-given gifts to aid those in need. A way that allows your family to learn about their faith and the path God has planned for them. A way to pray together as a family during day-to-day events and during traumatic moments that arise. A way to serve our family, friends, and community graciously knowing that holding on to our gifts prevents us from flourishing. A way to walk together to our ultimate goal—eternity together in heaven with God.

Remember, as parents and grandparents and godparents, you are the author of your story. If you ponder and realize you aren't on the correct course, no worries. Don't be afraid to alter your current faith steps. You can edit and tweak your story. You can even tear it up and start over. There is always time to make minor (or major) adjustments. Or, if you are pleased with the direction your family is taking regarding your faith, praise God and ask Him what is next. After all, discipleship never ends, and we can always expand in our knowledge and practice of our faith.

The goal is to never give up.

Allow living a life of stewardship to transform your family's story into the beautiful plan God created it to be.

I promise you will never regret it.

STEWARDSHIP PRAYER

Heavenly Father, we give You praise,
and thank You for the gift of our family.

Together, may we always remember that everything we
have is a gift from You. As we recognize Your infinite
generosity and unearned graces, may we strive to always
return our time, talent, and treasure to You in gratitude.

May our time together encourage us to grow as disciples,
may our hands and feet selflessly serve our ongoing needs,
and may our resources always help to build Your kingdom.

May our actions be done, not seeking reward, but in a Christ-like manner,
out of love, always imitating Your Heavenly ways.

I surrender our family to Your Heavenly will as
we seek to always serve You as faithful stewards.

AMEN.